Tasty and packed full of health benefits, these zero-proof drinks cover occasions of all kinds: a beautiful matcha latte to start the day; a nightcap for restful sleep; a showstopping punch for the dry bar at your holiday party; a hydrating ade; or a fun little sip, just because. Organized by season, these healthy drinks taste as good as you'll feel while sipping them.

everyday elixirs

everyday elixirs

Mocktails, Matchas, and Seasonal Drinks to Inspire Wellness

✦

Blair Horton

PHOTOGRAPHY BY JONI SCHRANTZ

HARVEST
An Imprint of WILLIAM MORROW

To my incredible community—
thank you for joining me on this Holistic Rendezvous. Your desire for this book inspired and pushed me to create it!

And to all who seek moments of nourishment, ritual, and joy—this book is for you.

recipes

syrups

spring

summer

fall

winter

introduction

What is your ideal drink? Or maybe you like to have different drinks for different occasions? Maybe water for hydration, a matcha or coffee for energy, and a special little drink just for fun? Are you looking to add small moments of self-care to your day? Because that's what these recipes are really about: starting your morning with a ritual, sharing pretty drinks at your get-together, winding down at night—all while adding in good-for-you ingredients in a fun and palatable way.

As a holistic nutrition consultant and natural chef, I've always sought ways to make nutrition and health feel both pleasurable and sustainable. People often assume that "getting healthy" means being rigid and restrictive—a party pooper if you will. But my approach has always been about abundance: adding in the good rather than fixating on taking away the bad. That mindset is the foundation of *Everyday Elixirs*.

My journey with elixirs actually began nearly a decade ago while studying holistic nutrition. Back then, I even wrote an e-book, *Teas, Tinctures, and Elixirs*, for my clients. Those drinks started as a personal ritual, a way to carve out a daily moment of nourishment just for me. So many clients shared how much they loved the ritual of their morning coffee, but since I've never been a coffee drinker (it makes me a little too energized), I began experimenting with herbs and functional ingredients to find my own moments of balance.

Over time, my creations evolved, blending my background and education in nutrition science with holistic nutrition, which also integrated principles from the thousands-year-old practice of traditional Chinese medicine (TCM). While somewhat different in practice, holistic nutrition and TCM share a foundational philosophy: Health is about the whole person, not just the food on your plate. Both traditions emphasize seasonal eating, balancing warming and cooling foods, and nourishing the body in alignment with nature's rhythms. You'll notice these principles throughout the book—except, of course, for the iced drinks (which TCM isn't a big fan of, but hey, balance!).

Fast-forward to today, and those early elixirs have evolved and grown with me. While I've refined and updated many of those original recipes, the essence remains the same. I still crave a warm cup of Relaxing Hot Chocolate (page 204) or a cozy but festive Simmer Pot Punch (page 212) as soon as the weather turns crisp. And what started as a nourishing practice for me has become the same for so many of you. That, to me, is the magic of these drinks.

Maybe you first picked up this book because you wanted more mocktail recipes after cutting back on alcohol. But these drinks provide so much more. These elixirs aren't just alcohol-free cocktails—they're acts of self-care and wellness. Developed with intention and backed by both nutrition science and ancient wisdom, each drink is crafted to support your body and mind. I didn't just remove alcohol from these drinks; I infused them with functional ingredients designed to uplift, relax, hydrate, and heal.

So whether you're seeking a moment of self-care, a way to celebrate without the aftermath of alcohol, or a vibrant and nourishing elixir, I hope you find the perfect sip to suit your needs. These drinks honor your body, uplift your spirit, and bring a little joy to your daily routine. My wish is that these recipes inspire you to create your own moments of ritual and celebration throughout the day.

Here's to vibrant health, delightful flavors, and the magic in every sip. Cheers!

Blair

mocktails for every season

I've always been deeply inspired by the fruits and vegetables of each season when it comes to cooking and creating beverages. A visit to the farmers' market, chatting with local farmers, and being drawn to the vibrant scents and colors of what's freshly available will always be my greatest source of inspiration. Not only is eating seasonally better for the environment and our bodies, but food at its peak ripeness—when it's bursting with flavor and nutrients—simply tastes the best.

That's why this book is organized by the seasons: spring, summer, fall, and winter. Each chapter celebrates the unique bounty of its time, offering recipes designed to reflect the ingredients and energy of that season.

In spring and summer, we're lucky to have an abundance of colorful, juicy fruits that take center stage in many of the recipes. Think vibrant berries, stone fruits, and refreshing melons that bring brightness to every sip. As the weather cools into fall and winter, I love leaning into the rich flavors of herbs, teas, and warming spices. These not only provide cozy, comforting drinks but also support our bodies in unique ways during colder months.

Seasonal eating and drinking is a powerful way to align with what your body naturally craves. In winter, for example, your body benefits from immunity-boosting ingredients like citrus loaded with vitamin C and warming herbs, such as ginger and cinnamon. Spring calls for lighter, detoxifying flavors, while summer is all about hydration and cooling ingredients. Fall, with its grounding spices and earthy tones, helps prepare the body for the slower, introspective energy of winter.

By following the seasons, you're not just making delicious drinks—you're nourishing your body with what it needs most at that moment. It's a simple yet profound way to connect with nature, support your health, and savor the flavors that shine brightest in each part of the year.

spring produce

✦

- CITRUS (lemons, limes, oranges, grapefruits, mandarins)
- STRAWBERRIES
- KIWI
- PINEAPPLE
- RHUBARB
- CHERRIES
- DRAGONFRUIT
- AVOCADO
- CARROTS
- GINGER
- MINT
- CILANTRO

summer produce

✦

- BERRIES (blueberries, raspberries, blackberries, strawberries)
- PEACHES
- PLUMS
- MELONS (watermelon, cantaloupe, honeydew)
- MANGOES
- PINEAPPLE
- PASSIONFRUIT
- CHERRIES
- CITRUS (lemons, limes)
- CUCUMBERS
- JALAPEÑO
- BASIL
- MINT
- CILANTRO
- THYME

fall produce

✦

- CITRUS (lemons, limes)
- FIGS
- GRAPES
- PERSIMMONS
- PUMPKINS
- APPLES
- PEARS
- PLUMS
- GINGER
- CILANTRO
- SAGE
- THYME
- ROSEMARY

winter produce

✦

- CITRUS (oranges, blood oranges, grapefruits, lemons, limes, mandarins, kumquats)
- POMEGRANATES
- CRANBERRIES
- ROSEMARY
- SAGE
- THYME
- GINGER

elevate your elixirs

If there's one piece of advice I can give you, it's this: Drop the rules. So many of us could benefit from embracing *play* and finding that childlike sense of creativity and wonder. When I create a recipe, I don't follow a strict formula. Instead, I focus on the ingredient I want to highlight or the benefits I'm after, and I let the flavors evolve until they taste just right for me.

Since no two people have the same palate, it's important to adjust drinks to suit your preferences. Want it sweeter, saltier, or brighter? Go for it! The same goes for presentation. Choose a glass that makes you happy—forget whether it's "right" for the drink. You'll also notice that I have suggestions for rims and garnishes for most of the recipes, not necessarily to add flavor or benefits but to elevate the drink and add a little something extra. Because we definitely drink with our eyes first!

Tools

I like to keep things simple, but there are a few tools that will make your life so much easier (and more fun)!

Cocktail Shaker: No need for anything fancy—a mason jar with a lid works great! Shaking is not only practical but stress relieving. Ever notice how animals "shake it off" after stress? Shaking helps release tension and energy. Plus, it aerates, froths, mixes, and chills your drink all at once.

Jigger: "Jigger" is just a fancy name for a shot glass or a small measuring cup. This will help you measure out your liquid and feel like a bartender!

Strainer: I use a strainer for syrups, juices, and certain drinks (but I honestly leave most of my drinks pretty pulpy because I love a drink that doubles as a snack). Having a cute cocktail strainer makes me feel cool, but again, it doesn't need to be fancy. Most people have fine-mesh strainers in their kitchens and this works too!

Citrus Juicer: Sure, you can hand-squeeze citrus, but a juicer saves time, gets more juice, and spares your hands from stings. Fresh citrus juice is nonnegotiable for a good drink!

Muddler: A muddler is perfect for smashing fruits and herbs to release their juices and flavors—and for letting out a little stress! I prefer a wooden muddler to avoid microplastics and because it is naturally antimicrobial.

Blender: A high-powered stand blender or immersion blender not only helps you make slushies and frozen drinks, but it's also a great way to make fresh juices without having to add another piece of equipment to your kitchen. You can blend up fresh fruit with a little water, then strain it through a fine-mesh sieve for a delicious juice.

Handheld Frother: This may not be something you use every day, unless you love making foamy matcha lattes like me, but it's a super helpful tool for quick mixing and frothing.

Kitchen Torch: Feeling fancy? While I don't use a kitchen torch often, it does make me feel really cool when I brûlée a marshmallow, a piece of citrus, or light an herb on fire for a smoky vibe. You absolutely do not need this, but again, we're being playful and this is really, really fun.

Garnishes

Nothing makes me feel more accomplished than a drink in my favorite glass with a beautiful garnish. I truly want you to feel proud when you make the drinks in this book. I want you to make yourself a nourishing beverage and look at it and feel transported to that giddy little place in your brain where you are happy, calm, and excited all at the same time. So you're not gonna skimp on the garnish, okay? I give you garnish options for each drink, but it can be as simple as a piece of dried citrus or as fancy as an edible flower.

Salt or Sugar with Citrus Rim

A salt or sugar rim is easy to do and uses every part of the citrus. It looks gorgeous while also tasting and smelling amazing.

2 tablespoons flaky salt or coarse-ground sugar

1 lime, lemon, or orange

Pour the salt or sugar onto a small plate. Zest your citrus over the top with a Microplane, making sure to avoid the bitter white part (the pith). Mix the zest with the salt or sugar. The rim mixture is ready to be used immediately. Alternatively, you can dry the mixture on a piece of parchment paper on the lowest setting in your oven for about an hour or until the zest is dry and crumbly. This allows it to store longer if you do not use it all.

To adhere the mixture to your glass, rub the flesh of a citrus slice along the rim of your glass, then roll the rim in the mixture. For extra sticking power and a little sweetness, you can brush the rim with a thin coating of honey instead of citrus juice.

Ice: I know ice may not seem like a garnish, but we all know a good ice cube when we see one. If you're making an iced beverage, don't skimp on the ice, okay? Okay. I know when you go to a bar or restaurant, you may think or say, "This drink is basically all ice," but there's a reason. You want to have enough ice to keep the drink so cold that the ice won't melt and water it down . . . unless you like that kind of thing. I also think ice can be a really fun place to get creative. Have some leftover fruit or herbs that are about to go bad? Cut them up and place them in an ice tray with water for some fun ice cubes. I love adding citrus, cucumbers, and herbs—you can get really creative.

Rims: There are so many ways to rim your glass and it really does elevate the vibes. Oftentimes, I add a fun rim for the looks, but it can also add a lot of flavor. My favorite rims usually include fresh citrus zest and salt. Throughout the book I give suggestions under the heading "Dress Your Glass," but feel free to get creative here.

Dehydrated Produce: I love dehydrated citrus as a garnish for my drinks; it really is my go-to. It just feels simple and classy. You can do this at home with a dehydrator or with your oven on the lowest setting. While citrus is the most common produce to dehydrate, you can also do this with pineapple, ginger, apples, pears, and rhubarb.

Seasonal Produce: It may seem obvious, but fresh fruit is the simplest garnish. You can skewer berries on a cocktail pick, make melon balls, slice apples or pears, add pineapple leaves, and even create ribbons out of cucumbers! The possibilities are endless, so play around with it!

Herbs: Fresh herbs not only look sleek and beautiful, but they also add aromatics. I actually have a huge mint bush planted right where I park at my house, so during the summer I always seem to touch it with my foot getting in the car, which brings the minty aroma into my car for the drive. It was definitely a happy accident, but you're going to purposely do this with your drinks. Smack some mint or basil and place it in your drink, so you can smell as you sip! I plant mint anywhere I want it to spread, but if you don't want it taking your garden over like a weed, make sure to plant it in its own pot!

Edible Flowers: The most elegant of all garnishes. When I have fresh flowers on my beverages, it always makes me smile. I even started curating my summer garden to grow edible flowers so that I could add them to food and beverages. Whether buying them or growing them yourself, make sure they are an edible type of flower and that they have not been treated with pesticides or chemicals. Here are some of my favorites: violet, viola, nasturtium, lavender, honeysuckle, marigold, rose, chamomile, hibiscus, calendula, pansy, borage, chive.

Glassware

As I mentioned earlier, I'm not a rule follower, and that's also true when it comes to glassware. Ice in a coupe glass? Sure! What matters is finding a glass you love—it truly elevates the drinking experience.

You don't need a huge collection—just pick glasses that bring you joy. I love thrifting for unique finds. Remember, you eat, or in this case drink, with your eyes first. A beautiful drink in a glass you adore will taste even better.

Herbs and Teas

Herbal teas are a huge part of many of my recipes. Not only are they a booster food—packed with vitamins, minerals, and nutrients—but they also add incredible depth of flavor. I know herbs can feel a little intimidating when you're first getting started, but I want to introduce them in a way that feels approachable.

First, let's talk about the difference between herbs and teas. This might feel a little in the weeds for a moment, but hey, it's important to be educated, right? Throughout this book, I refer to herbs, herbal

teas, and tea. The term "herb" covers a wide range of edibles like spices, flowers, barks, and leaves, whereas "tea" specifically refers to beverages made from the leaves of *Camellia sinensis*—aka the tea plant! Technically, many of the "teas" in this book are herbal infusions rather than true teas, but since we commonly refer to them as tea, I use that terminology for simplicity.

I personally love sourcing my herbs from local apothecaries because they offer a wide selection of culinary-grade herbs in both small and large quantities. It's a great way to buy just what you need for a recipe or to try something new without committing to a bulk size.

That said, I know this isn't an option for everyone. You can also order culinary-grade herbs online, but just note that they often come in larger bulk sizes. For a more accessible option, most grocery stores have tea sections where you can find many of these herbs in tea bags—especially some of the more familiar ones like chamomile, peppermint, and hibiscus.

Now that we've got that out of the way, let's dive into some of my favorite herbs and teas, which you'll find throughout the book. They are more than just flavorful additions—they offer powerful benefits that can enhance your health while making your drinks even more enjoyable!

Ginger: A warming root available fresh, dried, or powdered, ginger is a powerful anti-inflammatory and digestive aid, helping to reduce nausea, support gut health, and fight microbes. It also promotes circulation and immune support, making it great for balancing cold conditions in TCM.

Ceylon Cinnamon: Unlike common cassia cinnamon, Ceylon is milder and contains lower levels of coumarin.* It helps regulate blood sugar, has

* Coumarin can be harmful to the liver in high doses, so Ceylon cinnamon is safer to use for regular consumption.

antimicrobial properties, and adds a naturally sweet warmth to drinks.

Cardamom: A fragrant spice with digestive benefits, cardamom can help reduce bloating, freshen breath, and support respiratory health.

Rosemary: This aromatic herb supports memory, circulation, and digestion.

Thyme: A natural antimicrobial, thyme supports respiratory health and digestion.

Sage: Known for its cognitive benefits, sage supports brain function and hormonal balance.

Cloves: A warming spice with antimicrobial properties, cloves aid digestion and support oral health.

Turmeric: A powerful anti-inflammatory, turmeric supports joint health, digestion, and immune function.

Rose Petals: Aromatic and soothing, rose petals have calming properties, are rich in antioxidants, support skin health, and promote relaxation.

Rose Hips: A potent source of vitamin C, rose hips help boost immunity, support skin health, and reduce inflammation.

Hibiscus: Tart and vibrant, hibiscus is packed with antioxidants and supports heart health by helping regulate blood pressure.

Chamomile: Famous for its calming effects, chamomile aids digestion, reduces stress, and promotes restful sleep.

Lavender: Known for its soothing aroma, lavender helps alleviate stress, improve sleep, and support digestion.

Green Tea: High in catechins, green tea supports metabolism, brain function, and heart health while offering a mild caffeine lift.

Matcha: A form of powdered green tea with roots in Chinese and Japanese tea traditions, matcha is rich in antioxidants and provides a sustained energy boost. It supports brain function, promotes detoxification, and offers a calm focus thanks to its unique combination of caffeine and L-theanine.

Yerba Maté: A traditional South American tea known for its balanced energy boost, yerba maté provides caffeine along with vitamins, minerals, and antioxidants.

Earl Grey Tea: This black tea is infused with bergamot oil, which adds citrusy notes and may help reduce stress and support digestion.

Jasmine Tea: A fragrant tea often made with green tea leaves, jasmine has calming properties and is rich in antioxidants.

Red Raspberry Leaf: A well-known herb for women's health, red raspberry leaf supports hormone balance and reproductive health.

Butterfly Pea Flower: Vibrantly blue and packed with antioxidants, butterfly pea flower supports skin health and cognitive function while offering a fun color-changing effect.

Nettle: Rich in minerals like iron and calcium, nettle helps with allergies, detoxification, and overall nourishment. I use it dried, which can be found in tea bags or bulk, like other teas and herbs.

Maca: A root from the Andes known for its adaptogenic properties, maca helps support energy, stamina, and hormone balance.

Chaga: A medicinal mushroom rich in antioxidants, chaga supports immune health, reduces inflammation, and promotes overall vitality.

Bitters: Bitters are blends of herbs, roots, bark, and spices traditionally extracted in alcohol. Many bitters do contain alcohol, but there are also nonalcoholic versions depending on your preference. Bitters add depth, complexity, and a beautiful balance to drinks, especially by offsetting sweetness and enhancing digestion.

Some brands I love: Organic India teas, Traditional Medicinals teas, Yogi Tea, Numi Tea, All The Bitter, and Dram bitters.

Finally, although salt is of course not an herb, I want to mention it here because you'll notice it's often included as an ingredient in many of elixirs in this book. A pinch of mineral or sea salt not only brings out the flavors of the drinks, but it also adds electrolytes to keep you hydrated.

Syrups

✦

While I absolutely love a simple, no-fuss drink you can throw together without even turning on the stove, syrups bring a depth of flavor that can truly elevate your creations. Syrups are more than just sweeteners—they're an opportunity to infuse your drinks with vibrant flavors and functional benefits from health-supporting ingredients like herbs, spices, and fruits in a concentrated and versatile form. Plus, once you make a batch, you'll have a handy ingredient that can effortlessly transform any drink into something extraordinary.

Making syrups is an exercise in creativity. You can customize them to suit your taste, experimenting with flavors and sweetness levels (my recipes are lower in sugar than most). They're also wonderful for adding an extra layer of care and intention to your beverages. I think of them as little love notes in a bottle, ready to enhance every sip.

Whether you're crafting a cozy spiced chai syrup for winter lattes, a zesty ginger syrup for a refreshing spritz, or a delicate lavender syrup for floral springtime sips, these recipes are approachable, adaptable, and endlessly rewarding. And don't worry—I'll guide you through each step so you can feel confident experimenting and creating.

So let's dive into the world of syrups! I promise, once you try making your own, you'll wonder how you ever lived without them.

Ginger Honey Syrup

MAKES ABOUT 1 CUP

This may be my most made syrup because ginger is so good for you. It has anti-inflammatory, antiviral, and antibacterial properties, so even adding this syrup to warm teas is a simple way to soothe sore throats and colds. As a ginger lover, I think it tastes great in just about anything!

✦

⅓ cup sliced fresh ginger
Pinch of sea salt or mineral salt
½ cup honey

Place the ginger in a small saucepan, add 1 cup water and the salt and bring to a boil over medium-high heat.

Reduce the heat to low and simmer for 10 minutes.

Remove from the heat and let the mixture cool until warm. Stir in the honey until dissolved.

Blend the mixture in a stand blender or with an immersion blender, then strain through a fine-mesh sieve into a sealable container.

Storage

Allow to cool and then refrigerate for up to 2 weeks.

Tip

Don't toss your ginger pulp! I love adding this to stir-fries or baked goods!

Herbal Aperol Syrup

MAKES ABOUT 1 CUP

I worked so hard creating this Aperol alternative, and I love this syrup so much! Combine this syrup with herbal bitters for an Aperol dupe that is full of herbs that are also so good for you. These herbs are high in vitamin C and have calming properties, digestive benefits, and much more!

✦

2 tablespoons dried orange peel
2 tablespoons dried chamomile
2 tablespoons dried rose hips
1 tablespoon dried hibiscus
1 tablespoon vanilla bean paste
Pinch of sea salt or mineral salt
¼ cup honey

Combine the orange peel, chamomile, rose hips, hibiscus, vanilla bean paste, and salt in a medium saucepan and add 2 cups water. Bring to a boil over medium heat, then reduce to low heat and simmer for about 10 minutes, or until the liquid reduces to about 1 cup.

Strain through a fine-mesh sieve into a heatproof bowl. Discard the solids. Stir in the honey until dissolved.

Storage

Transfer to a sealable container and allow to cool. Refrigerate for up to 2 weeks.

Rose Syrup

MAKES ABOUT 1 CUP

No shade to rose water, but making your own rose syrup is way better! Plus, it has a stunning pink color, which I love, and it is high in vitamin C and thought to have heart-opening benefits as well. It has a beautiful lightly floral flavor, which I use in matchas, lattes, and many mocktails.

✦

¼ cup dried rose petals
Pinch of sea salt or mineral salt
½ cup honey or monk fruit sweetener

Bring 1 cup water to a boil in a small saucepan, then add the rose petals and salt and reduce the heat to low. Simmer for 10 minutes.

Remove from the heat and let the mixture cool until warm. Stir in the honey or sweetener until dissolved.

Strain through a fine-mesh sieve into a sealable container. Discard the solids.

Storage

Allow to cool and refrigerate for up to 2 weeks.

Rhubarb Syrup

MAKES ABOUT 1½ CUPS

This sweet-tart syrup is a lovely way to use rhubarb while it is in season. I always save the leftover rhubarb pulp to make muffins or bread. Rhubarb is rich in antioxidants and vitamin K, which are important for bone health.

✦

3 cups fresh or frozen chopped rhubarb
1 cup honey
Pinch of sea salt or mineral salt

Place the rhubarb in a medium saucepan, add 2 cups water plus the salt, and bring to a boil over medium heat.

Reduce the heat to low, cover, and simmer for 20 minutes.

Remove from the heat and let cool to warm. Stir in the honey until dissolved.

Strain through a fine-mesh sieve into a sealable container, reserving the pulp for baked goods, if desired.

Storage

Allow to cool and refrigerate for up to 2 weeks.

Dragonfruit Syrup

MAKES ABOUT 1 CUP

Vibrant with floral and tropical notes, this syrup is perfect for brightening any beverage. You can leave out the rose petals, but I love adding them in for their antioxidant and anti-inflammatory benefits.

✦

- ½ cup sweetener of choice, such as honey, allulose, monk fruit, or sugar
- ¼ cup chopped dragonfruit (frozen works well)
- 2 tablespoons dried rose petals (optional)
- Pinch of sea salt or mineral salt

Combine the sweetener, dragonfruit, rose petals (if using), and salt in a medium saucepan and add 1 cup water. Bring to a boil over medium heat, then reduce to low and simmer for 10 minutes.

Remove from the heat and let cool. Strain through a fine-mesh sieve into a sealable container. Discard the solids.

Storage

Allow to cool and refrigerate for up to 2 weeks.

Rosemary Thyme Syrup

MAKES ABOUT 1 CUP

This herbaceous syrup pairs beautifully with almost everything. Rosemary and thyme both have antimicrobial properties, making them great for the immune system, so I use this syrup the most during the fall and winter. One of my all-time favorite drinks is Rosemary Thyme Lemonade (page 132) because it is simple but still has a depth of flavor that makes it feel really special.

✦

½ cup honey or sweetener of choice
3 to 4 fresh rosemary sprigs
3 to 4 fresh thyme sprigs
Pinch of sea salt or mineral salt

Combine all the ingredients in a small saucepan, add 1 cup water, and bring to a boil over medium heat.

Reduce to a simmer and cook for 10 minutes.

Remove from the heat and let cool. Strain through a fine-mesh sieve into a sealable container. Discard the solids.

Storage

Allow to cool and refrigerate for up to 2 weeks.

Chai Syrup

MAKES ABOUT 1 CUP

This cozy syrup is a delightful addition to any drink. These spices are great for digestion and warming up your body in the colder months.

✦

3 cinnamon sticks

One 2- to 3-inch piece fresh ginger, sliced

2 tablespoons cardamom pods

1 tablespoon whole cloves

1 tablespoon fennel seeds

½ tablespoon black peppercorns

1 to 2 whole star anise

½ cup pure maple syrup

Pinch of sea salt or mineral salt

1 teaspoon pure vanilla extract, or 1 tablespoon vanilla bean paste

Slightly crush the cinnamon sticks, ginger, cardamom, cloves, fennel seeds, peppercorns, and star anise. You can use a mortar and pestle or a muddler. Toast in a medium saucepan over medium heat for 1 minute to release their aromas.

Add 1 cup water, the maple syrup, salt, and vanilla and bring to a boil. Reduce to a simmer and cook for 20 minutes.

Remove from the heat and let cool. Strain through a fine-mesh sieve into a sealable container. Discard the solids.

Storage

Allow to cool and refrigerate for up to 2 weeks.

Gingerbread Syrup

MAKES ABOUT 1 CUP

Pretty sure I captured the coziest gingerbread flavors in this syrup. I love using this in holiday drinks and lattes. Plus, it has the added anti-inflammatory, antiviral, and antibacterial benefits of ginger.

✦

- One 3- to 4-inch piece fresh ginger, sliced
- 3 cinnamon sticks
- 1 teaspoon whole cloves
- ½ teaspoon freshly grated nutmeg
- ⅓ cup coconut sugar
- 3 tablespoons molasses
- 1 teaspoon vanilla syrup, or 1 tablespoon vanilla bean paste
- Pinch of sea salt or mineral salt

Toast the ginger, cinnamon sticks, cloves, and nutmeg in a medium saucepan over medium heat for about 1 minute to release their aromas.

Add the sugar, molasses, vanilla, salt, and 1 cup water. Bring to a boil, then reduce the heat to low and simmer for 20 minutes.

Remove from the heat and let cool. Strain through a fine-mesh sieve into a sealable container. Discard the solids.

Storage

Allow to cool and refrigerate for up to 10 days.

Spring Bloom Syrup

MAKES ABOUT 1 CUP

This floral and herbaceous syrup is perfect for spring-inspired drinks. It is a bouquet of different dried flowers, with the addition of nettle for its natural antihistamine properties, which may help alleviate spring allergies. Hibiscus is high in vitamin C, which is also important for fighting off seasonal allergies, while rose, lavender, and chamomile add in calming properties. I also love the addition of calendula as it is known for benefiting skin health. And I know we all want an extra glow as we come out of hibernation from winter!

✦

- 1 tablespoon dried hibiscus
- 1 tablespoon dried chamomile
- 1 tablespoon dried calendula
- 1 tablespoon dried rose petals
- 1 tablespoon dried nettle
- 1 teaspoon dried lavender
- Pinch of sea salt or mineral salt
- ⅓ cup honey

Combine the hibiscus, chamomile, calendula, rose petals, nettle, lavender, and salt in a small saucepan and add 1 cup water. Bring to a simmer over medium heat and cook for 10 to 15 minutes.

Remove from the heat and let cool slightly. Stir in the honey until dissolved.

Strain through a fine-mesh sieve into a sealable container. Discard the solids.

Storage

Cool completely and refrigerate for up to 2 weeks.

Blueberry Syrup

MAKES ABOUT ½ CUP

This vibrant syrup highlights the natural sweetness of blueberries and has a stunning color.

✦

1 cup blueberries
¼ cup honey
Pinch of sea salt or mineral salt

Combine the blueberries, honey, and salt in a small saucepan, add ¼ cup water, and bring to a simmer over medium heat. Cook for 10 minutes, stirring occasionally.

Remove from the heat and let cool. Strain through a fine-mesh sieve into a sealable container. Discard the solids. Or, for a thicker syrup, blend in a stand blender or with an immersion blender.

Storage

Allow to cool and refrigerate for up to 2 weeks.

Strawberry Syrup

MAKES ABOUT ½ CUP

It's not just for the viral strawberry matcha latte (see page 80)—you can use this syrup in other lattes or mocktails as well.

1 cup hulled strawberries
¼ cup honey
Pinch of sea salt or mineral salt

Combine the strawberries, honey, and salt in a small saucepan, add ¼ cup water, and bring to a simmer over medium heat. Cook for 10 minutes, stirring occasionally.

Remove from the heat and let cool. Strain through a fine-mesh sieve into a sealable container. Discard the solids. Or, for a thicker syrup, blend in a stand blender or with an immersion blender.

Storage

Allow to cool and refrigerate for up to 2 weeks.

Spicy Peach Syrup

MAKES ABOUT 1 CUP

This fruity syrup is the main ingredient for the Spicy Ginger Peach Margarita (page 119), and it has a really lovely blend of spicy and sweet.

✦

2 ripe peaches, diced
One 2-inch piece fresh ginger, chopped
Pinch of red pepper flakes
Pinch of sea salt or mineral salt
⅓ cup honey

Combine the peaches, ginger, red pepper flakes, and salt in a medium saucepan and add 1 cup water. Bring to a simmer over medium heat and cook for 10 minutes.

Remove from the heat and stir in the honey. Blend in a stand blender or with an immersion blender until smooth.

Storage

Allow to cool and store in a sealed container in the refrigerator for up to 2 weeks.

Pumpkin Spice Syrup

MAKES ABOUT 1 CUP

A seasonal favorite, this syrup is perfect for lattes in the fall.

✦

⅓ cup pure maple syrup
¼ cup pumpkin puree
1 tablespoon pumpkin pie spice
1 tablespoon vanilla bean paste
Pinch of sea salt or mineral salt

Combine all the ingredients in a small saucepan, add 1 cup water, and bring to a simmer over medium heat. Reduce the heat to low and simmer for 10 minutes.

Remove from the heat and let cool.

Storage

Allow to cool and store in a sealed container in the refrigerator for up to 2 weeks.

Rose Hip Syrup

MAKES ABOUT 1 CUP

Rose hips are one of my favorite herbs because they are naturally sweet, with a slightly tart flavor. They are also full of vitamin C, so I love adding this syrup to teas as a sweetener if I'm not using it for a more thought-out drink.

✦

¼ cup dried rose hips
Pinch of sea salt or mineral salt
½ cup honey or monk fruit sweetener

Bring 1 cup water to a boil in a small saucepan. Add the rose hips and salt, then reduce the heat to low and simmer for 10 minutes.

Remove from the heat and let cool until warm. Stir in the honey or sweetener until dissolved.

Strain through a fine-mesh sieve into a sealable container. Discard the solids.

Storage

Allow to cool and refrigerate for up to 2 weeks.

spring

✦

Since spring is the season of new beginnings, there is no better place to start this book. I am a huge believer in cyclical living and connecting our bodies with nature, so I always think of spring as the true "new year" and the best time to set new intentions and goals—goals like incorporating more herbs in my diet, drinking more functional beverages, and trying out new recipes, of course!

In nature, we see radiant awakening and renewal in spring. Flowers are blooming and fruit trees begin to blossom—all this beauty popping up after the cold dormancy of winter. And just like these plants need more hydration, sun, and nutrients to reach their full potential, so do you! In TCM, spring is associated with the liver, the organ responsible for detoxification and maintaining a smooth flow of energy. Consider the season a time for "spring cleaning" your habits and your health.

With the new season, we naturally want to move our bodies more, spend time outside, and eat fresh and bright foods. Fruits like citrus, kiwi, pineapple, and strawberries support our body's natural detoxification systems while also hydrating us. They are high in vitamin C, which aids in the production of glutathione, a key antioxidant for detoxification and liver support. Their natural acidity also stimulates digestion, helping the body efficiently eliminate toxins. These fruits are also high in fiber and antioxidants, which are essential for elimination as well as energy and nutrient absorption.

Let these mocktails inspire you to sip in harmony with the spring season, honoring its promise of growth, vibrancy, and renewal. Cheers to spring and blooming into your best self!

Key Lime Pie Margarita

SERVES 1

This creamy and tangy drink makes me feel like I am sitting on the beach with a slice of key lime pie. At the same time, this drink feels completely nostalgic. I love going all out with a graham cracker rim to give it the full pie vibes. And yes, I know I'm not using actual key limes. Please feel free to, but it's an ingredient that most of us don't have access to at all times, and regular limes still give a fantastic flavor here!

✦

- Graham crackers, for the glass rim
- 1 teaspoon honey, plus more for the glass rim
- ¼ cup diced pineapple
- 2 ounces full-fat canned coconut milk
- Zest and juice of 1 lime (about 1 ounce juice)
- Pinch of sea salt or mineral salt
- Sparkling water

Crush the graham crackers into fine crumbs and spread them on a plate. Rub the honey along the rim of a glass, then dip the rim in the crumbs to coat. Set aside.

Combine the pineapple, coconut milk, lime zest and juice, 1 teaspoon honey, and the salt in a stand blender and blend until smooth.

Fill the prepared glass with ice, then pour the blended mixture over the ice.

Top with sparkling water and stir gently to combine.

Choose a Garnish

Add a dehydrated lime slice, fresh mint, and/or additional lime zest.

Strawberry Mandarin Shrub

SERVES 1

I have always loved finding ways to balance my blood sugar that are fun and delicious. This drink integrates apple cider vinegar in a delicious way that may also help balance your blood sugar, keeping energy levels stabilized.

✦

¼ cup diced strawberries
Juice of 2 mandarin oranges
1 tablespoon apple cider vinegar
Pinch of sea salt or mineral salt
Sparkling water
1 teaspoon honey (optional)

Muddle the strawberries, mandarin juice, apple cider vinegar, and salt in a glass until the strawberries are well mashed and the mixture is combined.

Fill the glass with ice, then top with sparkling water. Add the honey for additional sweetness, if desired. Stir gently to combine.

Choose a Garnish

Add a slice of fresh or dehydrated mandarin and/or sliced strawberries.

Dress Your Glass

Zest your mandarins and mix with flaky salt or try crushed freeze-dried strawberries. Rub the rim of the glass with a slice of lime or coat with honey before dipping into the rim mixture.

Kiwi Mint Mojito

SERVES 1

Did you know that kiwis actually have more potassium than a banana? Potassium is an essential mineral that is important for fluid and electrolyte balance, nerve function, and helping with muscle contractions—which is why a lot of people recommend bananas when someone has a cramp or charley horse. Kiwis are also super high in fiber and vitamin C, so this drink really packs an immune-boosting punch, is great for digestion, and is super refreshing.

✦

1 kiwi, peeled and diced
Juice of 1 lime (about 1 ounce juice)
1 teaspoon honey
Pinch of sea salt or mineral salt
4 to 5 fresh mint leaves
Sparkling water

Muddle the kiwi, lime juice, honey, salt, and mint leaves in a glass until the kiwi is mashed and the mint is aromatic.

Fill the glass with ice, then top with sparkling water. Stir well to combine.

Choose a Garnish

Add fresh mint leaves and a few slices of kiwi.

Dress Your Glass

Rim the glass with lime zest and flaky salt (see page 10).

Energizing Pineapple Teajito

SERVES 1

My sister likes to call herself "the kitchen magician," for her ability to throw random things together and create a masterpiece. Well, this drink was a kitchen magician moment for me because I just threw these ingredients together without a real plan. It seems almost too simple but has turned into a drink that I go back to over and over again! Pineapple juice is rich in bromelain, which supports digestion, while lime juice offers a burst of vitamin C for immune health. Green tea provides a gentle energy boost and is packed with antioxidants that promote focus and overall well-being.

✦

- 1 individual green tea bag
- 2 ounces hot water (175°F; see Note)
- 1½ ounces pure pineapple juice
- Juice of ½ lime (about ½ ounce juice)
- 1 teaspoon honey
- 4 to 5 fresh mint leaves
- Pinch of sea salt or mineral salt

Place the tea bag in a small bowl or measuring cup and add the hot water. Let steep for 2 to 3 minutes. Discard the tea bag and let the tea cool slightly.

Muddle the green tea, pineapple juice, lime juice, honey, mint leaves, and salt in a shaker to release the mint's aroma.

Add ice to the shaker and shake vigorously to mix and chill. Strain into a glass filled with fresh ice.

Choose a Garnish

Add fresh mint and pineapple leaves.

Dress Your Glass

Rim the glass with lime zest and flaky salt (see page 10).

Note

Boiling water can burn green tea leaves, so it's best to use hot water. I recommend a temperature of 175°F.

Carrot Cake Mocktail

SERVES 1

I am a *huge* fan of carrot cake because it has a lot of flavor, texture, and, of course, cream cheese icing. And since anything I love becomes inspiration, I created this creamy, spiced drink with the comforting flavors of carrot cake while delivering a nutrient-packed boost. Carrot juice provides a dose of vitamin A for healthy skin and eyes, while orange juice and coconut cream add immune-boosting vitamin C and healthy fats. The warming spices like cinnamon and ginger are known for their anti-inflammatory properties, making this a delicious and functional indulgence.

✦

- 2 ounces carrot juice
- 1½ ounces orange juice
- 1 ounce unsweetened coconut cream
- ¼ ounce lime juice
- 1 teaspoon vanilla bean paste
- Pinch of orange zest
- Pinch of ground Ceylon cinnamon
- Pinch of ground ginger
- Pinch of sea salt or mineral salt

Fill a shaker with ice, then add the carrot juice, orange juice, coconut cream, lime juice, vanilla bean paste, orange zest, cinnamon, ginger, and salt. Shake vigorously to mix and chill.

Strain into a glass filled with fresh ice.

Choose a Garnish

Add a dehydrated lime or orange slice, or both, for extra flair.

Dress Your Glass

Combine cinnamon and sugar, then use honey to coat the rim before dipping in the mixture.

Golden Glow Margarita

SERVES 2

This vibrant mocktail shines not only in appearance but also in its health benefits. Pineapple is rich in bromelain, a natural enzyme that supports digestion, while turmeric is a powerhouse for reducing inflammation and promoting overall wellness. Ginger honey syrup adds antioxidants and a touch of sweetness, making this a glowing beverage that's both refreshing and restorative.

✦

2 ounces pineapple puree or juice
1½ ounces Ginger Honey Syrup (page 24)
Juice of 1 lime (about 1 ounce juice)
¼ teaspoon ground turmeric
Pinch of sea salt or mineral salt
Pinch of freshly ground black pepper
Sparkling water or coconut water

Fill a shaker with ice, then add the pineapple puree, syrup, lime juice, turmeric, salt, and pepper. Shake vigorously to mix and chill.

Strain into glasses filled with fresh ice.

Top with sparkling water for a bubbly finish or coconut water for a smooth and tropical alternative.

Choose a Garnish

Add a lime wedge or pineapple slice for a tropical touch.

Dress Your Glass

Rim the glass with lime zest mixed with flaky salt (see page 10).

Hormone Happy Tripleade

SERVES 1

This vibrant citrus mocktail is a powerhouse of nutrients designed to support hormonal health. Citrus fruits like orange, grapefruit, and lime are rich in vitamin C, which is extremely important for ovulation and overall fertility. Kiwis are also high in vitamin C and may help with sleep because they contain serotonin, the precursor to melatonin, our sleep hormone. Nettle tea is known for its hormone-balancing properties by supporting the liver, which is responsible for detoxing excess hormones from the body.

✦

1 teaspoon dried nettle
2 ounces boiling water
Zest of ½ orange
Zest of ½ grapefruit
Zest of ½ lime
Flaky salt
Juice of ½ orange
Juice of ½ grapefruit
Juice of ½ lime (about ½ ounce juice)
1 kiwi, peeled and diced
Pinch of sea salt or mineral salt

Place the nettle in a small bowl or measuring cup and add the boiling water. Let steep for 10 minutes, then strain through a fine-mesh sieve into a shaker. Discard the solids. Set aside.

Mix together the orange, grapefruit, and lime zests in a small bowl. Combine half the zests with a pinch of flaky salt on a small plate. Wet the rim of a glass with water or some of the citrus juice, then dip the rim into the zest and salt mixture. Set aside.

Add the remaining zests, the orange juice, grapefruit juice, lime juice, kiwi, and sea salt to the shaker. Muddle well.

Add ice to the shaker and shake vigorously to mix and chill. Dirty pour the mixture (that is, pour the entire contents of your shaker, including ice, without straining) into the prepared glass and enjoy.

Choose a Garnish

Add a slice of any of the citruses used.

Rhubarb Retrograde

SERVES 1

Pair this drink with some upbeat nostalgic music and your favorite game for a groovy night in with your partner or friends. My personal favorites are Rummikub and Codenames. This drink is creamy and has some cozy flavors but is still slightly tart and energizing, which feels perfect for a night in with friends. Rhubarb is rich in vitamin K and antioxidants, while the spices add a comforting, anti-inflammatory touch.

✦

1½ ounces Rhubarb Syrup (page 27)
1 ounce unsweetened coconut cream
¼ ounce lime juice
2 pinches of ground Ceylon cinnamon
Pinch of sea salt or mineral salt
Pinch of ground cardamom

Fill a shaker with ice, then add all the ingredients. Shake vigorously to mix and chill.

Strain into a glass filled with fresh ice.

Choose a Garnish

Add a dehydrated lime slice. If you're feeling really fancy, try dehydrating rhubarb swirls.

Dress Your Glass

Rim the glass with lime zest mixed with flaky salt (see page 10).

Strawberry Rhubarb Sour

SERVES 1

This tangy and frothy mocktail features the classic pairing of strawberries and rhubarb. With aquafaba (the liquid from a can of chickpeas) or egg white for a velvety texture, this drink is a rich source of antioxidants and gut-friendly nutrients.

✦

¼ cup diced strawberries
1½ ounces Rhubarb Syrup (page 27)
¾ ounce lime juice
Pinch of sea salt or mineral salt
1 egg white, or 3 tablespoons aquafaba

Muddle the strawberries, syrup, lime juice, and salt in a shaker until the strawberries are well mashed.

Add the egg white, then fill the shaker with ice and shake vigorously until frothy.

Strain into a glass filled with fresh ice. For a chunkier version, dirty pour the mixture (that is, pour the entire contents of your shaker, including ice, without straining).

Choose a Garnish

Add a rhubarb swirl, dehydrated lime slice, and/or fresh strawberries.

Dress Your Glass

Rim the glass with lime zest mixed with flaky salt (see page 10).

Rose Lemonade

SERVES 1

I don't like to pick favorites, but this drink may just be one of them. This floral lemonade is packed with antioxidants and refreshing citrus flavors. The rose syrup offers a subtle, calming floral note, while smoked salt enhances the complexity of the drink. *And* it has a gorgeous pink hue that keeps me coming back for more!

✦

2 ounces Rose Syrup (page 26)
Juice of 1 lemon (about 1 ounce juice)
1 heaping teaspoon vanilla bean paste
Pinch of smoked sea salt
Sparkling water

Combine the syrup, lemon juice, vanilla bean paste, and salt in a shaker. Stir well to combine.

Pour into a glass filled with ice and top with sparkling water. Stir gently before serving.

Tip

For a still version, replace the sparkling water with 2 ounces of rose tea.

Dress Your Glass

I love mixing dried rose petals with salt or sugar for a stunning rim.

Ginger Pineapple Fizz

SERVES 1

This fizzy, tropical drink is loaded with functional benefits. Ginger aids digestion and inflammation, while apple cider vinegar supports gut health. Paired with pineapple juice for a burst of vitamin C, this mocktail is refreshing and rejuvenating.

✦

1 ounce Ginger Honey Syrup (page 24)
1 ounce pure pineapple juice
½ ounce apple cider vinegar
2 to 3 ounces sparkling water

Combine the syrup, pineapple juice, and apple cider vinegar in a glass. Stir to combine.

Add ice and top with sparkling water. Stir gently before serving.

Choose a Garnish

Add a sprig of rosemary for an aromatic touch.

Sleepytime Spritz

SERVES 1

When an Aperol spritz meets the sleepy girl mocktail, it becomes this Sleepytime Spritz! Tart cherry juice is a natural source of melatonin, while the herbal Aperol syrup adds calming herbal notes. Sparkling water provides a refreshing effervescence to complete this perfect bedtime spritz.

✦

3 ounces tart cherry juice
3 ounces sparkling water
1 ounce Herbal Aperol Syrup (page 25)

Combine the tart cherry juice, sparkling water, and syrup in a glass filled with ice. Stir gently to combine.

Choose a Garnish

Add an orange slice or a sprig of fresh rosemary for a touch of aromatics.

Kiwi Verdita

SERVES 3

Packed with hydrating and detoxifying ingredients, this vibrant drink is a blend of tropical and herbal flavors. Verditas are traditionally served as a palate cleanser between tequila tastings in Mexico and are known for being green and herbaceous, which is my kind of drink! Pineapple offers digestion support, kiwi provides a boost of vitamin C, and cucumber and cilantro support hydration and detoxification.

✦

2 cups chopped pineapple
2 kiwis, peeled and chopped
1 small cucumber, chopped
Bunch of fresh cilantro
Handful of fresh mint leaves
Juice of 4 limes (about 4 ounces juice)
Sparkling water (optional)

Place all the ingredients in a stand blender and blend until smooth.

Strain through a fine-mesh sieve into a large container. Discard the solids.

Divide the juice among three glasses. Serve as is or top with sparkling water for added fizz.

Storage

Store the strained juice in a sealed container in the refrigerator for 3 to 4 days.

Tip

For additional sweetness, stir in some honey. If desired, adjust with more lime juice for extra brightness.

Choose a Garnish

Add a dehydrated lime slice.

Dress Your Glass

Rim the glass with lime zest mixed with flaky salt (see page 10).

Pink Pony Princess

SERVES 1

It's the summer of 2024 and the song "Pink Pony Club" is constantly stuck in your head, so you make it your entire personality, including in this pink drink. This strikingly vibrant mocktail balances the bitterness of grapefruit with the herbaceous complexity of rosemary and thyme. The addition of green tea provides a gentle energy boost, making it a perfect afternoon drink. Even after all this time, this drink (and the song) is still a hit!

✦

1 individual green tea bag

2 ounces hot water (175°F; see Note on page 48)

2½ ounces pure grapefruit juice

¾ ounce Rosemary Thyme Syrup (page 29)

¾ ounce Dragonfruit Syrup (page 28)

Juice of ½ lime (about ½ ounce juice)

Place the tea bag in a small bowl or measuring cup and add the hot water. Let steep for 2 to 3 minutes. Discard the tea bag and let the tea cool slightly.

Fill a shaker with ice, then add the cooled tea, grapefruit juice, both syrups, and the lime juice. Shake vigorously to mix and chill.

Strain into a glass and serve.

Tip

For a caffeine-free version, replace the green tea with sparkling water.

Dress Your Glass

For a stunning rim, combine grapefruit zest with flaky salt and some dried rose petals! Rub the rim with a slice of grapefruit or coat with honey before dipping into the mixture.

Spring Sangria

SERVES 4

A refreshing and hydrating mocktail perfect for gatherings, this sangria is loaded with antioxidants from green tea and vitamin C from fresh fruit. Coconut water adds electrolytes, making it both delicious and nourishing.

✦

- 2 individual green tea bags, or 2 teaspoons loose-leaf green tea
- 4 ounces hot water (175°F; see Note on page 48)
- 1 cup pure pineapple juice
- 1 cup coconut water
- Juice of 2 limes (about 2 ounces juice)
- 1 cup sliced strawberries
- ½ cup sliced pineapple
- 1 orange, sliced
- 1 lime, sliced
- Large pinch of sea salt or mineral salt
- Sparkling water

Place the tea bags in a small bowl or measuring cup and add the hot water. Let steep for 2 to 3 minutes. Discard the tea bags and let the tea cool. Transfer the tea to a large pitcher. If using loose-leaf tea, strain through a fine-mesh sieve directly into the pitcher and let the tea cool there. Discard the solids.

Add the pineapple juice, coconut water, lime juice, strawberries, pineapple, orange, lime, and salt. Stir well.

To serve, pour the sangria into glasses filled with ice and top with sparkling water for a fizzy finish.

Choose a Garnish

Add a slice of citrus or strawberry, or even pineapple leaves!

Electrolyte Recovery Drink

SERVES 2 TO 3

This hydrating and nourishing beverage mimics the electrolyte balance of traditional sports drinks with a natural twist. Coconut water replenishes electrolytes, citrus juices provide vitamin C, and mineral salt supports hydration. Add your choice of colorful powders for a visual and functional boost! Pitaya powder is loaded with antioxidants, vitamins (especially vitamin C), and minerals. Blue spirulina is considered a superfood due to its high vitamin (especially B vitamins) and mineral content as well as antioxidant and anti-inflammatory properties. Beet powder is known for being high in nitrates, enhancing oxygen delivery to muscles, which basically means it can be helpful for athletic performance. Butterfly pea flower, which looks blue but turns a purply-pink color when it interacts with citrus, is known for being high in antioxidants and helping reduce stress.

✦

1 cup coconut water

Juice of 2 oranges, such as blood orange, Cara Cara, navel, or Valencia

Juice of 2 limes (about 2 ounces juice)

Large pinch of sea salt or mineral salt

1 teaspoon pitaya powder (pink), blue spirulina (blue), beet powder (reddish pink), or butterfly pea flower (purple), for color (optional)

Combine the coconut water, orange juice, lime juice, salt, and your powder of choice (if using) in a shaker. Add 1 cup water and shake vigorously to mix and dissolve the salt.

Divide among glasses filled with ice and enjoy a refreshing, colorful drink.

Tip

Customize the flavor and function by experimenting with different citrus varieties and powders. This is also a great recipe to sneak in inner fillet aloe vera juice for skin health and digestive benefits.

Mandarin Mojito

SERVES 1

When Cuties are in season, you have to make this cutie mocktail! This vibrant and zesty drink is packed with vitamin C from mandarin and lime juices, while mint and a pinch of salt add a refreshing and restorative touch.

✦

Juice of 2 mandarins
Juice of ½ lime (about ½ ounce juice)
1 mandarin, sliced into pieces (skin on)
About 10 fresh mint leaves
½ teaspoon honey
Pinch of sea salt or mineral salt
Sparkling water

Muddle the mandarin juice, lime juice, mandarin slices, mint leaves, honey, and salt in a glass to release the flavors.

Fill the glass with ice and top with sparkling water. Stir gently.

Choose a Garnish

Add fresh mint leaves and a fresh or dehydrated mandarin slice.

Dress Your Glass

Brush the rim with honey or rub with a slice of lime or mandarin, then dip in flaky salt mixed with mandarin and lime zest (see page 10).

Spring Bloom

SERVES 1

This drink is a functional powerhouse. The herbs in the syrup—hibiscus, chamomile, calendula, rose petals, and nettle—support seasonal allergies, glowing skin, and immune health. You just combine with sparkling or still water for a delicious, restorative beverage!

✦

1 ounce Spring Bloom Syrup (page 32)
4 ounces sparkling or still water
¼ ounce lime or lemon juice (optional)
1 ounce coconut water (optional)

Mix together the syrup and water in a glass with ice for a light floral beverage.

If desired, for a more balanced option, add the lime juice and coconut water.

Choose a Garnish

Add an edible flower to keep with the theme!

Avocado Margarita

SERVES 1

There is a restaurant in Denver called Alma Fonda Fina that has one of the most well-known avocado margaritas in town—after trying a sip I knew I had to re-create it for this book! Creamy avocado and bright citrus come together in this luxurious and nutrient-packed mocktail. Avocado offers heart-healthy fats, while lime and orange juices provide antioxidants and hydration.

✦

½ small ripe avocado
Juice of 1 lime (about 1 ounce juice)
2 ounces orange juice or mandarin juice
1 ounce coconut water
1 teaspoon honey
Pinch of smoked sea salt
A few slices of jalapeño (optional, but a great add-in if you prefer it spicy)

Muddle the avocado, lime juice, orange juice, coconut water, honey, salt, and the jalapeños (if using) in a shaker until blended.

Add ice and shake vigorously until smooth.

Strain into a glass filled with fresh ice.

Tip

For a smoother texture or when batching, blend the ingredients instead of shaking.

Choose a Garnish

Garnish with a dried lime slice.

Dress Your Glass

For extra flair, rim your glass with Tajín seasoning or go for a standard rim, with lime zest mixed with flaky salt (see page 10).

Strawberry Matcha
with Cardamom Rose Cold Foam

SERVES 1

This elegant drink combines earthy matcha with sweet strawberry syrup and a luxurious cardamom rose foam. Matcha is a nutrient-dense green tea powder known for its unique health benefits, which come from its rich concentration of antioxidants, catechins, and the calming compound L-theanine. I consider it my daily superfood and love getting creative with the flavor profile—like taking your "standard" strawberry matcha and adding a cardamom rose cold foam!

✦

¼ cup hot water (165°F)

1 teaspoon ceremonial-grade matcha powder

1 teaspoon honey

2 tablespoons heavy cream, half-and-half, or plant-based cream

1 teaspoon vanilla bean paste

¼ teaspoon rose water

¼ teaspoon ground cardamom

Pinch of sea salt or mineral salt

1 to 2 ounces Strawberry Syrup (page 34)

4 ounces milk of choice, such as Cashew Milk (page 92)

Whisk together the hot water, matcha, and honey in a small bowl until slightly frothy. Set aside.

In another small bowl, whisk together the heavy cream, vanilla bean paste, rose water, cardamom, and salt. Froth until thick and creamy. Set aside.

Pour the syrup into a glass. This is your base. Add ice, if desired.

Pour the milk over the syrup base. Pour the matcha mixture on top of the milk layer.

Top with the cardamom rose cold foam and serve immediately.

Choose a Garnish

Garnish with dried rose petals or crushed freeze-dried strawberries.

Summer

I'm usually not one to choose favorites, but when it comes to seasons, summer always wins. Yes, it gets *hot*, but farmers' markets are thriving, fruit is abundant (even here, in Colorado!), and there's nothing better than the freedom of wearing shorts or skirts all season long—hands down the comfiest attire, in my opinion.

In TCM, summer is the season of yang energy. Yang is symbolized by the sun: active, expansive, and full of vitality and growth. This vibrant energy brings joy, laughter, and connection, but when there's too much heat in the body, it can leave you feeling depleted and drained.

That's why summer is all about staying cool, hydrated, and balancing the fire with water (yin). To help you make the most of this powerful energy, these drinks are designed to be light, hydrating, and cooling. Juicy fruits like melons, cucumbers, and peaches help hydrate and cool, while ingredients like coconut water replenish lost minerals and offer a boost of potassium and magnesium.

These drinks aren't just refreshing—they also create space for a calm moment in the midst of all the summer hustle. They allow you to balance yang energy with a moment of stillness, serenity, and pure enjoyment.

Heatwave Hydrator

SERVES 1

This recipe is scientifically backed to cool you off! Have you noticed that spicy foods are more popular in warmer regions of the world? That's because the spice actually helps to cool you off! In this drink, watermelon provides hydration with its high water content, lime juice offers a zesty vitamin C boost, and jalapeño adds a metabolism-boosting and cooling kick. This recipe also uses sumac, which has a tart and tangy flavor and is used in Middle Eastern cuisine. It is traditionally used as a digestive aid, but since it is rich in antioxidants, it has many other benefits as well!

✦

½ cup cubed watermelon
Juice of 1 lime (about 1 ounce juice)
¼ teaspoon sumac
½ teaspoon vanilla bean paste
A few slices of jalapeño
Sparkling water

Muddle the watermelon, lime juice, sumac, vanilla bean paste, and jalapeño slices in a glass to release the flavors.

Add ice and top with sparkling water. Stir gently and enjoy.

Choose a Garnish

Add a dehydrated lime slice or a small slice of watermelon.

Dress Your Glass

Lime zest mixed with flaky salt (see page 10) is a fun rim, but you can also replace the lime zest with sumac. Rub the rim with a slice of lime or coat with honey before dipping in your preferred mixture.

Hydrating Watermelon Sangria

SERVES 6 TO 8

No one wants their friends getting dehydrated, so this is a great mocktail to serve at any of your summer gatherings! Packed with fresh fruit and hydrating coconut water, this sangria is the ultimate summer party drink. Watermelon provides electrolytes, while the medley of berries and mint adds antioxidants and a refreshing burst of flavor.

✦

4 cups cubed watermelon
2 cups coconut water
Juice of 4 limes (about 4 ounces juice)
Pinch of sea salt or mineral salt
1 peach, sliced
½ cup cherries, pitted and halved
⅓ cup strawberries, sliced
¼ cup raspberries
¼ cup blueberries
Large handful of fresh mint leaves
Sparkling water, ginger beer, or zero-proof sparkling wine

Place the watermelon cubes, coconut water, lime juice, and salt in a stand blender and blend until smooth.

Transfer the watermelon mixture to a large pitcher and add the peach slices, cherries, strawberries, raspberries, blueberries, and mint leaves. Stir well.

To serve, fill glasses with ice, pour the sangria mixture over the ice, and top with your preferred sparkling beverage.

Choose a Garnish

This is a fun one for a garnish bar! You can add fresh mint leaves, lime slices, jalapeño slices, cherries, or a watermelon slice.

Blueberry Matcha
with Strawberry Cold Foam

SERVES 1

People are always captivated by the beauty of a blueberry matcha, but we can make it even more fun by adding a strawberry cold foam. As a berry girl, I will use any excuse to put multiple berries in a recipe, and this layered beverage, as stunning as it is delicious, is no exception. Plus, I love the benefits matcha provides—a boost of antioxidants and gentle energy.

✦

¼ cup hot water (165°F)
1 teaspoon ceremonial-grade matcha powder
1 ounce Blueberry Syrup (page 33)
4 ounces Cashew Milk (recipe follows)
2 tablespoons heavy cream or half-and-half
2 teaspoons freeze-dried strawberry powder

Whisk together the hot water and matcha in a small bowl until frothy.

Pour the syrup into a glass. This is your base. Fill the glass with ice (optional).

Pour the cashew milk over the syrup base.

Pour the whisked matcha on top of the milk layer.

In another small bowl or measuring cup, froth the heavy cream with the freeze-dried strawberry powder. Spoon over the matcha and serve.

Tip

Layering the drink creates a stunning presentation, but stirring before sipping ensures all flavors are perfectly balanced.

Choose a Garnish

Top with more freeze-dried strawberry powder.

CASHEW MILK

MAKES 4 CUPS

⅓ cup raw cashews
2 cups filtered water
1 tablespoon vanilla bean paste
Pinch of sea salt or mineral salt

Blend the cashews, water, vanilla bean paste, and salt in a stand blender until smooth. If desired, for a smoother texture, strain the mixture through a clean sieve into a jar with a lid.

Storage

Store in an airtight container in the refrigerator for 3 to 5 days.

Strawberry Cardamom Rose

SERVES 1

Cardamom and rose are a match made in flavor heaven. The calming and beautifying properties of rose petals with grounding cardamom pairs perfectly with the sweetness and antioxidant power of strawberries.

✦

1 tablespoon rose petals
3 ounces boiling water
¼ cup strawberries
Juice of 1 lime (about 1 ounce juice)
1 teaspoon vanilla bean paste
Pinch of ground cardamom

Place the rose petals in a small bowl or measuring cup and add the boiling water. Let steep for 10 minutes, then strain through a fine-mesh sieve into a shaker. Discard the solids.

Add the strawberries, lime juice, vanilla bean paste, and cardamom to the shaker. Muddle well to release the strawberries' flavor.

Add ice and shake vigorously to mix and chill.

Strain into a glass filled with fresh ice. For a chunkier version, dirty pour the mixture (that is, pour the entire contents of your shaker, including ice, without straining).

Choose a Garnish

Add fresh strawberries to a skewer and place in the drink, or skip the skewer altogether and place a strawberry slice on top.

Dress Your Glass

Combine dried rose petals with flaky salt or sugar for a beautiful rim! Rub the rim with a slice of lime or coat with honey before dipping in the mixture.

Raspberry Hibiscus Sour

SERVES 2

If you've ever placed raspberries on the tips of your fingers and then eaten them off (like most people do with Bugles), then this recipe is for you! This tangy and vibrant sour is rich in antioxidants from hibiscus and raspberries, while the egg white creates a velvety texture for a sophisticated mocktail experience.

✦

1 tablespoon dried hibiscus
4 ounces boiling water
½ cup fresh or frozen raspberries, thawed if frozen
Juice of 2 limes (about 2 ounces juice)
½ tablespoon vanilla bean paste
Pinch of sea salt or mineral salt
1 egg white, or 2 tablespoons aquafaba (the liquid from a can of chickpeas)

Place the hibiscus in a small bowl and add the boiling water. Let steep for 10 minutes, then strain through a fine-mesh sieve into a glass. Set aside. Discard the solids.

Muddle the raspberries in a shaker until well mashed.

Add the strained tea, lime juice, vanilla bean paste, salt, and egg white to the shaker.

Dry shake (that is, shake without ice—this step is important to create the foam), then add ice and shake again to chill.

Strain into two glasses filled with ice.

Choose a Garnish

Add a skewer with raspberries or a dehydrated lime slice.

Dress Your Glass

Use a mortar and pestle or spice grinder to combine hibiscus with flaky salt or coarse sugar. Rub the rim with a slice of lime or coat with honey before dipping in the mixture.

Lavender Blueberry Bliss

SERVES 1

Confession: I'm not always the biggest fan of lavender in a drink and find it can be too overpowering with excessive floral and bitter notes, but blueberries may just be its perfect complement. This calming drink combines antioxidant-rich blueberries with the relaxing properties of lavender for a perfect pairing of flavors and benefits!

✦

¼ cup blueberries
1 teaspoon dried lavender, or 1 individual lavender tea bag
2 ounces boiling water
Juice of ½ lemon (about ½ ounce juice)
½ teaspoon vanilla bean paste
Pinch of sea salt or mineral salt
Sparkling water

Place the blueberries in a shaker.

Place the lavender in a small bowl or measuring cup and add the boiling water. Let steep for 10 minutes, then strain the tea through a fine-mesh sieve over the blueberries. Discard the solids.

Add the lemon juice, vanilla bean paste, and salt. Muddle well.

Add ice and shake vigorously to mix and chill.

Strain into a glass filled with fresh ice and top with sparkling water.

Choose a Garnish

Add a few fresh blueberries, a dehydrated lemon slice, or a sprig of lavender for a visual and aromatic boost.

Dress Your Glass

I like lemon zest mixed with flaky salt (see page 10) or dried lavender or lavender flowers mixed with salt or coarse sugar. Rub the rim with a slice of lime or coat with honey before dipping in the mixture.

Cucumber Passion Matcha Margarita

SERVES 1

I have matcha in some capacity almost every day, but sometimes I want it with a twist. This hydrating and energizing mocktail combines the antioxidants of matcha with the cooling properties of cucumber and a tropical passionfruit twist. It's energizing, hydrating, and refreshing!

✦

- 2 tablespoons hot water (165°F)
- 2 teaspoons honey
- ¼ teaspoon ceremonial-grade matcha powder
- Pinch of sea salt or mineral salt
- 4 cubes frozen passionfruit juice, or pulp from 1 fresh passionfruit
- Juice of 1 lime (about 1 ounce juice)
- ¼ cup cubed peeled cucumber
- A few slices of jalapeño
- Sparkling water (optional)

Whisk together the hot water, honey, matcha, and salt in a small bowl until the matcha is frothy. Add the passionfruit cubes to melt into the mixture.

Muddle the lime juice, cucumber cubes, and jalapeño slices in a shaker until well mashed.

Add the matcha mixture and ice. Shake vigorously to mix and chill.

Strain into a glass filled with fresh ice. Top with sparkling water, if desired.

Choose a Garnish

Add a dehydrated lime slice, a cucumber twirl, or half of a passionfruit.

Dress Your Glass

Rub the rim with a slice of lime or coat with honey before dipping in lime zest mixed with flaky salt (see page 10).

Plum Mojito Smash

SERVES 1

Sometimes a delicious drink really is as simple as highlighting a seasonal fruit. This juicy, herbaceous mocktail combines hydrating plums with the refreshing flavors of lime and mint. Plums offer a dose of antioxidants and vitamin C, while mint adds a cooling touch, making it ideal for warm days.

✦

¼ cup diced plums
Juice of 1 lime (about 1 ounce juice)
2 teaspoons honey
Pinch of sea salt or mineral salt
4 to 5 mint leaves
2 ounces sparkling water or brewed lemongrass tea

Muddle the plums, lime juice, honey, salt, and mint leaves in a shaker to release the flavors.

Add ice to the shaker and shake vigorously to mix and chill.

Strain into a glass filled with fresh ice.

Top with the sparkling water or lemongrass tea for a fragrant twist.

Choose a Garnish

Add a sprig of mint and/or plum slices.

Dress Your Glass

Rub the rim with a slice of lime or coat with honey before dipping in lime zest mixed with flaky salt (see page 10).

Rosemary Cherry Shrub Spritzer

SERVES 1, WITH EXTRA SHRUB

This tangy shrub combines sweet cherries with the woodsy aroma of rosemary for a sophisticated beverage base. Cherries provide antioxidants like anthocyanins, while apple cider vinegar supports gut health.

✦

SHRUB (MAKES ABOUT 1 CUP)

1 cup fresh or frozen pitted cherries, thawed if frozen

¼ cup honey

¼ cup apple cider vinegar

3 to 4 fresh rosemary sprigs

1 tablespoon vanilla bean paste

Sparkling water or ginger beer

Make the shrub: Muddle the cherries, honey, apple cider vinegar, rosemary, and vanilla bean paste in a small bowl to mash the cherries and release the rosemary's flavor.

Strain through a fine-mesh sieve into a sealable container. Discard the solids.

Cover and store in the refrigerator for at least 3 days or up to 1 week.

When ready to use, pour 1 ounce of the shrub in a glass filled with ice. Add sparkling water or ginger beer and mix for a tangy and refreshing drink.

Tip

You can even use the shrub in salad dressings or marinades!

Dress Your Glass

Coat the rim with honey before dipping into rosemary salt/sugar or coconut sugar.

Cherry Limeade

SERVES 1

I was absolutely obsessed with the Sonic drive-in as a kid. The roller-skating servers, the window trays, the pebble ice, and, most importantly, the Cherry Limeades. This *Everyday Elixirs* version upgrades the classic with vibrant flavors and health benefits. Black cherries deliver antioxidants like anthocyanins for heart and anti-inflammatory support, while lime juice adds immune-boosting vitamin C and zesty freshness. I also love subbing cherries for strawberries for a strawberry limeade as well!

✦

- Zest of 1 lime
- Flaky salt
- ¼ cup fresh or frozen pitted cherries, thawed if frozen (thawed cherries are juicier)
- Juice of 1 lime (about 1 ounce juice)
- 1 teaspoon honey
- Pinch of sea salt or mineral salt
- Sparkling water

Mix the lime zest with a pinch of the flaky salt on a small plate. Wet the rim of a glass with water or lime juice, then dip it into the lime salt to coat.

Muddle the cherries, lime juice, honey, and sea salt in a shaker until well mashed.

Fill the prepared glass with ice, then pour the muddled mixture over it.

Top with sparkling water and stir gently.

Tip

For a smoother version, blend the cherries, lime juice, and honey in a stand blender, then pour over ice and top with sparkling water.

Choose a Garnish

Add a lime slice and a cherry.

Dress Your Glass

Rub the rim with a slice of lime or coat with honey before dipping in lime zest mixed with flaky salt (see page 10).

The Melon Volley

SERVES 1

In the past few years, I've become a bit of a tennis fan and player, so I had to riff on the infamous Honey Deuce that is served at the U.S. Open each year. This famous drink has lemonade, vodka, raspberry liqueur and is iconic for its melon balls that mimic tennis balls. This nonalcoholic version combines honeydew melon, yerba maté tea, and raspberries for a drink that's as functional as it is delicious. Honeydew juice and raspberries provide a dose of antioxidants, while yerba maté offers a natural energy boost—perfect for sipping courtside or after a match.

✦

1 individual yerba maté tea bag
4 ounces hot water (175°; see Note on page 48)
¼ cup raspberries
Juice of 1½ lemons (about 1½ ounces juice)
2 teaspoons honey
Pinch of sea salt or mineral salt
1 honeydew melon, halved and seeded
Sparkling water
Fresh mint sprig

Place the tea bag in a small bowl or measuring cup and add the hot water. Let steep for 3 to 5 minutes and let cool.

Muddle the raspberries, lemon juice, honey, salt, and brewed tea in a shaker to release the raspberries' flavors.

Use a melon baller to make your "tennis balls." Extra juice will be created during this step, which is what I use in the recipe. I just pour it out of the half melon into a cup. Alternatively, you can blend a cup of honeydew melon and strain to create your own juice. You will want 1 ounce of melon juice. Set aside the melon balls and add the melon juice to the shaker.

Add ice to the shaker and shake vigorously.

Strain into a glass filled with fresh ice. For a chunkier version, dirty pour the mixture (that is, pour the entire contents of your shaker, including ice, without straining).

Top with sparkling water and garnish with melon balls and a mint sprig.

Spicy Mango Margarita

SERVES 1

I love this summer drink because it tastes delicious and comes together so easily. It's the perfect balance of sweet, spicy, and zesty flavors. Mango puree provides a hydrating dose of vitamins A and C, supporting skin health and immune function. Jalapeño adds capsaicin, which boosts metabolism, promotes heart health, and supports digestion. Lime juice adds antioxidants and vitamin C, making this drink both refreshing and functional.

- ⅓ mango, peeled and chopped
- A few slices of jalapeño
- Juice of 1 lime (about 1 ounce juice)
- 1 teaspoon honey
- Pinch of sea salt or mineral salt
- Sparkling water

Place the mango in a small bowl and blend with an immersion blender until smooth and pureed.

Add the jalapeño slices, lime juice, honey, and salt. Muddle to release the jalapeño's spice.

Fill a glass with ice, add the spiced mango, and top with sparkling water. Stir gently before serving.

Choose a Garnish

Add a lime wheel and a slice of jalapeno for an extra kick.

Dress Your Glass

Rub the rim with a slice of lime or coat with honey before dipping in lime zest mixed with flaky salt (see page 10).

Raspberry Rose Margarita

SERVES 1

This mocktail pairs the tart brightness of raspberries with the floral elegance of rose syrup. Raspberries are rich in antioxidants and vitamin C, supporting immune health and skin vitality. Rose syrup adds calming and beautifying properties, while sparkling water provides a refreshing effervescence. The rose-petal sugar rim enhances the presentation, making it a delightful treat for the senses.

✦

¼ cup fresh or frozen raspberries, thawed if frozen

Juice of 1 lime (about 1 ounce juice)

1 ounce Rose Syrup (page 26)

Pinch of sea salt or mineral salt

Sparkling water

Muddle the raspberries, lime juice, syrup, and salt in a shaker to release the raspberries' juices.

Fill a glass with ice, then pour the mixture over it. Top with sparkling water and stir gently.

Choose a Garnish

Add fresh raspberries to a skewer and/or add a dehydrated lime slice.

Dress Your Glass

Rub the rim with a slice of lime or coat with honey before dipping in coarse sugar mixed with dried rose petals.

Blue Hawaiian Mocktail

SERVES 1

Originally created in Waikiki, Hawaii, by head bartender Harry Yee, the Blue Hawaiian is a vibrant tropical cocktail, thanks to blue curaçao liqueur. This mocktail version is just as vibrant and uses a special ingredient to create this stunning color naturally: blue spirulina, which not only gives it a beautiful hue but also adds a nutrient boost because it is packed with vitamins, minerals, and antioxidants.

✦

2 ounces full-fat canned coconut milk
Juice of ½ lime (about ½ ounce juice)
Juice of ½ lemon (about ½ ounce juice)
½ cup pineapple chunks
½ teaspoon blue spirulina powder

Add all ingredients to a blender and blend until smooth and creamy. Pour over ice and enjoy! Alternatively, you could use 1.5 oz pineapple juice instead of pineapple chunks and just shake with ice in a shaker.

Choose a Garnish

Add edible flowers, pineapple leaves, and/or a slice of pineapple for a tropical finish!

Blackberry Hibiscus Margarita

SERVES 1

I am of the mind that you can turn just about any fruit into a delicious margarita. This is a tangy and floral twist on a classic margarita, featuring antioxidant-packed blackberries and the refreshing tartness of hibiscus tea.

✦

- 1 tablespoon dried hibiscus flowers
- 3 ounces boiling water
- ⅓ cup blackberries
- ¾ ounce lime juice
- 1 teaspoon vanilla bean paste or honey
- Pinch of sea salt or mineral salt

Place the hibiscus flowers in a small bowl or measuring cup and add the boiling water. Let steep for 5 to 10 minutes, then strain through a fine-mesh sieve into a glass. Set aside. Discard the solids.

Muddle the blackberries, lime juice, vanilla bean paste, and salt in a shaker to release the blackberries' juices.

Add the steeped hibiscus tea, fill the shaker with ice, and shake vigorously to mix and chill.

Strain into a glass filled with fresh ice. For a chunkier version, dirty pour the mixture (that is, pour the entire contents of your shaker, including ice, without straining).

Choose a Garnish

Add a lime wedge and/or a skewer of blackberries.

Dress Your Glass

Rub the rim with a slice of lime or coat with honey before dipping in lime zest mixed with flaky salt (see page 10). I also love macerating hibiscus and combining it with flaky salt or sugar.

Spicy Ginger Peach Margarita

SERVES 1

In the summer of 2018, I had the pleasing realization that the home I had purchased came with a peach tree. This meant I needed numerous ways to use and enjoy my home-grown peaches in all their glory. This spicy-sweet mocktail combines juicy peach, zesty lime, and the warmth of ginger for a delightful burst of flavor.

✦

2 ounces Spicy Peach Syrup (page 35)
Juice of ½ lime (about ½ ounce juice)
Sparkling water

Combine the syrup and lime juice in a glass and stir well. Add ice and top with sparkling water.

Choose a Garnish

Add a slice of dehydrated lime and ginger, or a lime wedge and a slice of peach.

Dress Your Glass

Rub the rim with a slice of lime or coat with honey before dipping in lime zest mixed with flaky salt (see page 10) or Tajín seasoning.

Jasmine Cantaloupe Blossom

SERVES 1

If you're looking for a drink that feels delicate and feminine and will nourish your skin from the inside out, this is it. The scent of jasmine immediately feels calming, and its polyphenols are great for protecting the skin. And the cantaloupe provides hydration and is rich in beta-carotene and vitamin C, supporting glowing skin and immune health.

✦

½ tablespoon dried jasmine
2 ounces boiling water
About 1 cup chopped cantaloupe
¾ ounce Ginger Honey Syrup (page 24)
Juice of ½ lime (about ½ ounce juice)
Pinch of sea salt or mineral salt

Place the jasmine in a small bowl or measuring cup and add the boiling water. Let steep for 10 minutes, then strain through a fine-mesh sieve into a glass. Set aside. Discard the solids.

Meanwhile, make your cantaloupe puree: Blend the cantaloupe in a stand blender until smooth.

Fill a shaker with ice, then add the cantaloupe puree, jasmine tea, syrup, lime juice, and salt. Add ice and shake vigorously to mix and chill.

Strain into a glass filled with fresh ice.

Choose a Garnish

Add cantaloupe balls to a skewer and fresh mint leaves.

Dress Your Glass

Rub the rim with a slice of lime or coat with honey before dipping in lime zest mixed with flaky salt (see page 10).

Calming Cantaloupe Cooler

SERVES 2

Nothing is better than a slushie during the summer, and this one is designed to be soothing at the end of a hot summer day. It's got hydrating ingredients like cantaloupe and cucumber juice, plus calming chamomile and aloe vera juice. Aloe vera juice has lots of benefits for the digestive system and skin health, but I personally don't love the taste, so I add it to elixirs that hide the taste but still give me the benefits!

✦

1 tablespoon dried chamomile flowers
3 ounces boiling water
3 cups frozen cantaloupe chunks
Juice of 2 limes (about 2 ounces juice)
2 ounces aloe vera juice (see Note)
2 ounces cucumber juice or filtered water

Place the chamomile flowers in a small bowl or measuring cup and add the boiling water. Let steep for 5 to 7 minutes, until the water turns a deep yellow. Strain through a fine-mesh sieve into a stand blender.

Add the frozen cantaloupe, lime juice, aloe vera juice, and cucumber juice and blend until smooth.

Serve in glasses with a lime salt rim for extra flavor.

Choose a Garnish

Add a slice of cantaloupe, melon balls, and/or a dehydrated lime slice.

Dress Your Glass

Rub the rim with a slice of lime or coat with honey before dipping in lime zest mixed with flaky salt (see page 10).

Note

I buy preservative-free inner fillet aloe vera juice.

Energizing Frozen Tropical Margarita

SERVES 2

This frozen tropical mocktail combines mango, pineapple, and green tea for a refreshing and invigorating treat. Mango and pineapple are rich in enzymes that aid digestion and are loaded with vitamin C to boost immunity. Green tea adds a gentle dose of caffeine and antioxidants like catechins, which support metabolism and brain function. Lime juice provides a zesty burst of flavor and additional immune support, while the salt helps replenish electrolytes.

✦

- 1 individual green tea bag
- 4 ounces hot water (175°F; see Note on page 48)
- 1 cup frozen mango chunks
- 1 cup frozen pineapple chunks
- Juice of 1½ limes (about 1½ ounces juice)
- Pinch of sea salt or mineral salt

Place the tea bag in a small bowl or measuring cup and add the hot water. Let steep for 2 to 3 minutes, then discard the tea bag, and pour into a stand blender and let cool.

Add the mango, pineapple, lime juice, and salt and blend until smooth and creamy.

Divide between two glasses and be refreshed!

Choose a Garnish

Add a dehydrated lime slice and pineapple leaves.

Dress Your Glass

Rub the rim with a slice of lime or coat with honey before dipping in Tajín seasoning.

Cucumber Cooler

SERVES 1

This hydrating and restorative mocktail features cucumber, aloe vera, and ginger for a wellness-packed drink. Cucumber juice provides electrolytes and supports hydration, while aloe vera juice soothes digestion and enhances skin health. Lime juice is rich in antioxidants and vitamin C, and ginger aids in reducing inflammation and improving digestion, making this drink both functional and delicious.

✦

- 1 large cucumber
- 3 to 4 fresh mint leaves
- Juice of 1 lime (about 1 ounce juice)
- 1 ounce aloe vera juice (see Note)
- 1 ounce Ginger Honey Syrup (page 24)
- Pinch of sea salt or mineral salt

Place the cucumber in a stand blender and blend to liquify. Strain through a fine-mesh sieve into a small bowl to extract the juice. Discard the solids.

Muddle the mint leaves and lime juice in a shaker, then add 3 ounces of the cucumber juice (see Tip), the aloe vera juice, syrup, and salt. Add ice and shake vigorously to mix and chill.

Strain into a glass filled with fresh ice.

Tip

Store any extra cucumber juice in a sealed container in the refrigerator for up to 24 hours.

Choose a Garnish

Lean into green and add a sprig of mint and/or a shaved cucumber ribbon or two.

Dress Your Glass

Rub the rim with a slice of lime or coat with honey before dipping in lime zest mixed with flaky salt (see page 10).

Note

I buy preservative-free inner fillet aloe vera juice.

fall

As someone who thinks of herself as energetic and ambitious, I feel a slight sense of sadness when I start to feel the crisp air of fall. It signals the start of slowing down, shorter days, and turning inward—things that can be a little challenging for an extroverted perfectionist like me. But every year, I remind myself that this is the natural time to chill out and embrace the rhythm of moving a bit slower. Fall is the season to unwind and reflect, giving us permission to rest and nourish ourselves.

In TCM, fall is associated with the lungs and the element of metal, which represents structure, boundaries, and clarity. The lungs are deeply connected to both breath and emotion, making this a powerful time to support respiratory health and release grief. It's a time to let go of what no longer serves us, just as the trees shed their leaves. This season invites us to pause, replenish, and restore.

These fall-inspired recipes are designed to hydrate, warm, and soothe while supporting your body's natural rhythms. They're not just a cozy treat but also a celebration of what's in season and a reminder that it's time to slow down. Think comforting and grounding spices like cinnamon and ginger and immune-boosting apples and pears. I still get a kick out of foraging for apples all over the city every year. It's been a highlight of living in Denver in the fall. Maybe go apple picking to make Spiced Hibiscus Apple Punch (page 155) or snuggle up with a book and cozy chai elixir. Allow these mocktails to guide you into the beauty of fall, a time for nourishing warmth, rejuvenation, and gratitude.

Rosemary Thyme Lemonade

SERVES 1

I created this recipe a few years ago for Halloween, but I honestly want to drink it year-round. This lemonade is more than just refreshing—it's packed with functional benefits. Rosemary and thyme are rich in antioxidants and anti-inflammatory compounds that support cognitive function and digestion, while lemon juice provides immune-boosting vitamin C.

A pinch of charcoal adds a detoxifying element plus a spooky vibe. But please note that it can decrease the effectiveness of some medications, so feel free to leave it out.

✦

1 ounce Rosemary Thyme Syrup (page 29)
Juice of 1 lemon (about 1 ounce juice)
Pinch of salt
Pinch of activated charcoal (optional)
Sparkling water

Combine the syrup, lemon juice, salt, and charcoal (if using) in a glass. Stir well to mix.

Fill the glass with ice and top with sparkling water. Stir gently to combine.

Choose a Garnish

Add a sprig of fresh rosemary and thyme and a dehydrated lemon slice for a polished presentation.

Dress Your Glass

Rub the rim with a slice of lime or coat with honey before dipping in lime zest mixed with flaky salt (see page 10).

Aromatic Ginger Fizz

SERVES 2

If you grew up similar to the way I did, ginger ale was the prescribed medicine for any stomachache because we knew that ginger was great for our bellies. I still love a fizzy ginger drink and this one is super aromatic and invigorating. It's packed with ginger for a zingy drink that's great for digestion and your immune system—no stomachache required!

✦

Zest of 1 lime
Flaky salt
Two 2-inch pieces fresh ginger, finely grated
¼ cup full-fat canned coconut milk
Juice of 1 lime (about 1 ounce juice)
1 tablespoon honey
Pinch of sea salt or mineral salt
Sparkling water

Mix the lime zest with a pinch of the flaky salt on a small plate. Wet the rims of two glasses and dip them into the lime salt to coat.

Combine the ginger, coconut milk, lime juice, honey, and salt in a small bowl. Stir until well mixed.

Fill the prepared glasses with ice and divide the mixture evenly between them.

Top with sparkling water and stir gently.

Choose a Garnish

Add a slice of ginger, a dehydrated lime slice, and a dehydrated lime swirl.

Dress Your Glass

Rub the rim with a slice of lime or coat with honey before dipping in lime zest mixed with flaky salt (see page 10).

Apple Cider Margarita

SERVES 1

An apple cider marg without fall's best friend, apple cider? I know, I'd better explain myself. Most apple ciders are loaded with sugar, so we are using fresh apple juice and chai spices to get the apple cider flavor. *But:* This apple cider marg is really all about the addition of apple cider vinegar. It doesn't overpower the other flavors we've got going on in this drink and it adds some digestive benefits (and so does the chai syrup!). Plus, apple cider vinegar can be beneficial for blood sugar balance when consumed before a high carb or sugary meal. So maybe this drink and some apple cider donuts?

✦

3 ounces pure apple juice
1 ounce Chai Syrup (page 30)
¾ ounce lime juice
1 tablespoon apple cider vinegar
Sparkling water

Fill a shaker with ice, then add the apple juice, syrup, lime juice, and apple cider vinegar. Shake vigorously to mix and chill.

Strain into a glass filled with fresh ice.

Top with sparkling water and stir gently to combine.

Choose a Garnish

Add an apple slice, a cinnamon stick, and/or a star anise for a warm, seasonal presentation.

Dress Your Glass

Coat the rim with honey, then dip in cinnamon sugar.

The Matsuhisa

SERVES 1, WITH EXTRA SYRUP

A couple of years ago I was visiting Aspen and stumbled into Matsuhisa, an acclaimed Japanese sushi restaurant. We asked for the staff's favorites and they said we had to try the Gardener cocktail . . . and it was *incredible*. It's a vibrant green drink that is herbaceous, slightly sweet, and has a kick of spice. So I took those flavors and created an alcohol-free version that you can drink every day! This recipe will make a big batch of syrup, but you'll be glad it did, since you're going to love this fresh drink!

✦

HERBACEOUS SYRUP
(MAKES ABOUT 1½ CUPS)
2 bunches fresh cilantro
1 green apple, cored and chopped
1 serrano pepper, seeds removed
⅓ cup honey
Juice of 2 limes (about 2 ounces juice)
Pinch of sea salt or mineral salt

Juice of 1 lime (about 1 ounce juice)
Sparkling water

Make the syrup: Place the cilantro, apple, serrano pepper, honey, lime juice, and salt in a stand blender, add 1½ cups water, and blend until smooth.

Strain through a fine-mesh sieve or cheesecloth into a sealable container. Discard the solids. You can store this syrup in the refrigerator for 3 to 4 days.

To serve, fill a glass with ice, then add 2 ounces of the syrup and the lime juice. Top with sparkling water. Stir gently to mix.

Choose a Garnish

Add a dehydrated lime slice, serrano slices, and even edible flowers.

Dress Your Glass

Rub the rim of the glass with a slice of lime or coat with honey before dipping in black salt.

Plum Cobbler

SERVES 1, WITH EXTRA COMPOTE

This versatile drink delivers cozy, spiced comfort in every sip. I wanted it to elicit a plum cobbler, which we know tastes amazing both hot from the oven and, the next day, cold from the fridge. Plums are rich in antioxidants like vitamin C and polyphenols, which support immune health and reduce inflammation. Ginger promotes digestion and reduces nausea, while cinnamon and cardamom add warming anti-inflammatory properties.

✦

PLUM COMPOTE
(MAKES ABOUT ½ CUP)

½ cup diced plums

One 1-inch piece fresh ginger, sliced

1 tablespoon honey or sweetener of choice

½ teaspoon ground Ceylon cinnamon

Pinch of ground cardamom

Pinch of sea salt or mineral salt

Boiling water or sparkling water

Make the compote: Combine ¼ cup room-temperature water, the plums, ginger, honey, cinnamon, cardamom, and salt in a small pot over medium heat. Bring to a simmer and cook until the plums have broken down, 10 to 15 minutes.

Remove from the heat and let cool. Remove and discard the ginger slices and mash the remaining mixture with a fork or blend. For a smoother texture, strain through a fine-mesh sieve and discard the solids.

Serve hot or cold: For a hot drink, mix 2 ounces of the compote with ⅓ cup boiling water in a mug. For a cold version, fill a glass with ice, add 2 ounces of the compote, and top with sparkling water.

Choose a Garnish

Add a cinnamon stick and/or a slice of plum for a polished presentation.

Creamy Spiced Rose Hip Elixir

SERVES 1

Creamy elixirs are my love language because they feel like a hug in a cup. I love adding coconut milk for this effect because it has healthy fats for brain and energy support. This creamy elixir combines rose hips with warming spices for a fall drink packed with vitamin C to boost immunity and skin health.

✦

1 tablespoon dried rose hips
3 ounces boiling water
½ ounce full-fat canned coconut milk
1 teaspoon vanilla bean paste
Pinch of ground cardamom
Pinch of ground Ceylon cinnamon
Pinch of sea salt or mineral salt

Place the rose hips in a small bowl or measuring cup and add the boiling water. Let steep for at least 20 minutes.

Fill a shaker with ice. Strain the rose hips through a fine-mesh sieve into the shaker. Discard the solids.

Add the coconut milk, vanilla bean paste, cardamom, cinnamon, and salt. Shake vigorously to mix well and chill.

Strain into a glass filled with fresh ice.

Choose a Garnish

Add a cinnamon stick!

Hibiscus Twist

SERVES 1

Hibiscus is one of my all-time favorite teas because it is vibrant in taste and color. It's an herb that pretty much everyone can get on board with on its own, which is great since it is rich in anthocyanins, which support cardiovascular health and lower blood pressure. Since this is a fall drink, I balanced the tart and uplifting flavor with the warming and comforting spices of ginger, cinnamon, and cardamom for all the cozy fall vibes.

✦

1 tablespoon dried hibiscus
5 ounces boiling water
1 teaspoon vanilla bean paste
1 teaspoon honey
⅛ teaspoon ground Ceylon cinnamon
⅛ teaspoon ground ginger
Pinch of ground cardamom
Pinch of sea salt or mineral salt

Place the hibiscus in a small bowl or measuring cup and add the boiling water. Let steep for 20 minutes.

Fill a shaker with ice. Strain the hibiscus through a fine-mesh sieve into the shaker. Discard the solids.

Add the vanilla bean paste, honey, cinnamon, ginger, cardamom, and salt. Shake vigorously to mix and chill.

Strain into a glass filled with fresh ice.

Choose a Garnish

Add a cinnamon stick and/or a slice of ginger. Candied ginger on a skewer also makes a fun garnish!

Dress Your Glass

For a vibrant, fun glass, coat the rim with honey, then dip in a mixture of ground hibiscus and coarse sugar.

Raspberry PMS Soother

SERVES 1

I designed this soothing drink to be consumed the week before your period and during menstruation to help with cramping and overall uterine health. The gingery syrup can be helpful if you are experiencing cramping. I love adding Ceylon cinnamon because it can balance blood sugar and it has anti-inflammatory properties as well.

✦

½ tablespoon dried red raspberry leaf tea
2 ounces boiling water
¼ cup raspberries
¾ ounce lemon juice
½ ounce Ginger Honey Syrup (page 24)
⅛ teaspoon ground Ceylon cinnamon

Place the red raspberry leaf tea in a small bowl or measuring cup and add the boiling water. Let steep for 20 minutes, then strain through a fine-mesh sieve into a glass. Discard the solids.

Muddle the raspberries in a shaker, then add the lemon juice, syrup, cinnamon, and strained tea. Add ice and shake vigorously to chill.

Strain into a glass filled with fresh ice. For a chunkier version, dirty pour the mixture (that is, pour the entire contents of your shaker, including ice, without straining).

Choose a Garnish

Add fresh raspberries and a twist of lemon peel for a visually appealing and functional garnish.

Cinnamon Spice and Everything Nice

SERVES 1

This comforting drink is a powerhouse of warming spices and immune-boosting ingredients, perfect for chilly days or when you need a wellness boost. Cinnamon is rich in antioxidants like polyphenols, which help reduce inflammation and stabilize blood sugar levels. Ginger adds digestive support and anti-inflammatory properties, while rose hips are loaded with vitamin C to promote skin health and strengthen immunity.

✦

- 1 tablespoon dried cinnamon tea (ideally Ceylon cinnamon tea)
- 6 ounces boiling water
- ½ ounce Rose Hip Syrup (page 37)
- ½ ounce Ginger Honey Syrup (page 24)
- Juice of ½ lemon (about ½ ounce juice)
- Sparkling water (optional)

Place the cinnamon tea in a small bowl or measuring cup and add the boiling water. Steep for at least 15 minutes, then strain through a fine-mesh sieve into a glass. Discard the solids.

Stir in both syrups and the lemon juice.

Pour into a mug to serve hot. For a cold version, pour into an ice-filled glass and top with sparkling water.

Choose a Garnish

Add a lemon slice and a cinnamon stick for a festive touch.

Pear and Sage Tea Tonic

SERVES 1, WITH EXTRA COMPOTE

Pears and sage are two underrated ingredients and they happen to go well together. I love this drink iced or warm depending on the variable fall-morning temperatures. It's lightly energizing from the Earl Grey tea, but bergamot is great for stress reduction and the sage adds some calming benefits as well.

✦

PEAR AND SAGE COMPOTE (MAKES ABOUT 1 CUP)

1 ripe pear, cored and chopped

4 to 5 sage leaves

⅓ cup pure maple syrup

Pinch of sea salt or mineral salt

1 individual Earl Grey tea bag, or 1 teaspoon loose-leaf tea

3 ounces boiling water

Juice of ½ lime (about ½ ounce juice)

Make the compote: Combine the pear, sage, maple syrup, and salt in a small saucepan over medium heat. Add ¾ cup water and simmer for 10 minutes.

Once cooled, use an immersion blender (or transfer to a stand blender) to blend until smooth.

Place the tea bag in a small bowl or measuring cup and add the boiling water. Let steep for 3 to 5 minutes, then discard the tea bag.

Combine the prepared tea, 2 ounces of the compote, and the lime juice in a mug. For a cold version, add these ingredients to an ice-filled glass and gently stir.

Storage

Store the leftover compote in the fridge for 3 to 4 days.

Choose a Garnish

Add a sage sprig or a slice of pear for a stunning finish!

Dress Your Glass

Coat the rim with honey, then dip in coarse sugar.

Pear and Ginger Spritz

SERVES 1

This refreshing spritz combines the natural sweetness of pear juice with the spicy warmth of ginger for a hydrating and digestion-supporting beverage. Pear juice, thanks to its fiber and antioxidants, aids in digestion and heart health, while ginger provides anti-inflammatory, immune-boosting benefits and also promotes healthy digestion.

✦

- 1 ripe pear, cored and chopped
- 1 ounce Ginger Honey Syrup (page 24)
- ¾ ounce lime juice
- 2 ounces sparkling water

Place the pear in a stand blender and blend until smooth, then transfer to a glass. For a thinner juice, blend with ¼ cup water, then strain though a fine-mesh sieve into a glass.

Add the syrup and lime juice to the glass. Stir well. Add ice and top with the sparkling water.

Choose a Garnish

Add slices of fresh or dried pear.

Dress Your Glass

Rub the rim with a slice of lime or coat with honey before dipping in lime zest mixed with coarse sugar.

Spiced Hibiscus Apple Punch

SERVES 4

Nothing screams fall to me like sipping cider at an orchard or bonfire, but I'll be honest: Most ciders are a bit too sweet for me. This festive punch combines the sweet warmth of apple juice and spices with tangy hibiscus. Hibiscus supports cardiovascular health and reduces inflammation, while apple juice provides hydration and immune-boosting vitamin C. Warming spices like cinnamon, ginger, and cloves enhance circulation, improve digestion, and add a cozy, aromatic touch. This recipe is for a cold punch, but you could serve it warm if you prefer.

✦

- 2 tablespoons dried hibiscus
- 2 cups boiling water
- 1 cup pure apple juice
- Juice of 1 lemon (about 1 ounce juice)
- ½ teaspoon ground Ceylon cinnamon
- ½ teaspoon ground ginger
- ¼ teaspoon ground cloves
- Sparkling water

Place the hibiscus in a small bowl or measuring cup and add the boiling water. Steep for 5 to 7 minutes, then strain through a fine-mesh sieve into a glass. Discard the solids. Cool and refrigerate.

Combine the chilled tea, apple juice, lemon juice, cinnamon, ginger, and cloves in a pitcher with ice. Stir well.

Divide among four glasses over ice, then top each with sparkling water.

Choose a Garnish

Garnish with apple slices and cinnamon sticks.

Creamy Pumpkin Pie Matcha
with Rosemary Thyme Cold Foam

SERVES 1

If you're craving dessert in a glass that is full of the comforting flavor of pumpkin pie, this drink is for you! Pumpkin is rich in beta-carotene, supporting skin and eye health, while black tea adds antioxidants and a gentle energy boost. Orange and lime juices provide a burst of vitamin C for immunity, and a dash of bitters aids digestion.

✦

¼ cup hot water (165°F)
1 teaspoon ceremonial-grade matcha powder
2 tablespoons heavy cream, half-and half, or plant-based cream
¾ ounce Rosemary Thyme Syrup (page 29)
1½ ounces Pumpkin Spice Syrup (page 36)
4 ounces milk of choice (I love cashew milk, page 92)

Whisk together the hot water and matcha in a small bowl until slightly frothy. Set aside.

In another small bowl, use a handheld frother to froth the heavy cream and rosemary thyme syrup until thick and creamy. Set aside.

Pour the pumpkin spice syrup into a glass. This is your base. Add ice.

Pour your milk of choice over the pumpkin pie syrup base. Pour the whisked matcha on top of the milk layer. Top with the rosemary thyme cold foam and serve immediately.

Cozy Chai Elixir

SERVES 1

Chai is basically a hug in a cup for your body and soul. Chai spices like cinnamon, ginger, and cardamom promote digestion, reduce inflammation, and can even help with bloating. Coconut milk adds healthy fats to support brain health and energy, while the syrup soothes the throat and boosts immunity.

✦

2 individual chai tea bags (see Note)
4 ounces boiling water
2 ounces full-fat canned coconut milk
1 ounce Ginger Honey Syrup (page 24)
Pinch of sea salt or mineral salt

Place the tea bags in a small bowl or measuring cup and add the boiling water. Let steep for 5 to 7 minutes. Discard the tea bags.

Serve hot for comfort or cold for a refreshing twist. For a hot drink, combine the freshly brewed tea, coconut milk, syrup, and salt in a mug and stir well. For a cold version, cool the tea and then pour all ingredients in a glass filled with ice and stir well.

Choose a Garnish

Garnish with a cinnamon stick and/or star anise.

Note

Instead of tea bags, you can use 1 ounce of Chai Syrup (page 30).

Apple Spice

SERVES 2

This spiced apple drink is the ultimate fall comfort, packed with the warming spices of the season. Apples provide fiber and vitamin C for immune support, while ginger and cinnamon improve digestion and reduce inflammation. Cloves add antibacterial properties, and a pinch of cayenne, while optional, offers a metabolism-boosting kick.

✦

2 cinnamon sticks
1 cup chopped apples
One 2-inch piece fresh ginger, sliced
2 to 3 whole cloves
Pinch of cayenne pepper (optional)
Pinch of sea salt or mineral salt
2 tablespoons honey

Combine the cinnamon sticks, apples, ginger, cloves, cayenne (if using), and salt in a small saucepan over medium heat. Add 1 cup water and simmer for about 15 minutes or until the apples begin to break down, enjoying the aroma as it doubles as a simmer pot.

Carefully remove the cinnamon sticks and cloves. Transfer the remaining mixture to a blender, add the honey, and blend. Strain through a fine-mesh sieve into two glasses filled with ice. Discard the solids.

Top with sparkling water and give it a stir.

Choose a Garnish

Garnish with a cinnamon stick and a slice of apple, because who doesn't love a snack with their drink!

Dress Your Glass

Coat the rim with honey before dipping in coarse sugar.

Applerol Spritz

SERVES 1

This refreshing mocktail combines the crispness of apple juice with the herbal depth of the Aperol-inspired syrup. Apple juice offers hydration and vitamin C, while the syrup infuses flavors from orange peel, chamomile, hibiscus, and rose hips, which are known for their calming, immune-boosting, and antioxidant properties. The spices of cinnamon and ginger add a metabolism-boosting kick.

✦

1 ounce pure apple juice
1 ounce Herbal Aperol Syrup (page 25)
2 ounces sparkling water
Pinch of ground Ceylon cinnamon
Pinch of ground ginger

Combine the apple juice, syrup, sparkling water, cinnamon, and ginger in an ice-filled glass. Stir well and enjoy.

Tip

For a more festive option, swap out the sparkling water for nonalcoholic sparkling wine or champagne.

Choose a Garnish

Apple slices and a cinnamon stick finish this drink with a fresh, aromatic touch.

Fig and Ginger Sparkler

SERVES 1

Figs always signal to me the end of summer and the beginning of fall. They're high in fiber and antioxidants and promote digestive and heart health, too. To capture the feeling I get picking figs at my friends' beach house, I devised this drink to be bright and energizing with just a hint of fall vibes from the ginger, which also aids in reducing inflammation, easing nausea, and improving circulation.

✦

1 individual green tea bag
2 ounces hot water (175°F; see Note on page 48)
2 large fresh figs, diced (about ¼ cup)
1 ounce Ginger Honey Syrup (page 24)
¾ ounce lemon juice
Pinch of sea salt or mineral salt
Sparkling water

Place the tea bag in a small bowl or measuring cup and add the hot water. Let steep for 2 to 3 minutes. Discard the tea bag.

Place the figs in a shaker, then add the tea, syrup, lemon juice, and salt. Muddle well.

Strain into a glass filled with ice and top with sparkling water.

Choose a Garnish

Add a slice of lemon, a slice of ginger, a fig slice, and/or a sprig of mint for a finishing touch.

Pecan Pie No-tini

SERVES 2

This rich and creamy mocktail captures the comforting flavors of pecan pie in mocktini form. Pecans are high in heart-healthy fats, antioxidants, and minerals like magnesium, which support heart health and reduce inflammation. Maple syrup provides natural sweetness along with energy-boosting properties. The warming spices of cinnamon and nutmeg offer digestive support and a cozy, aromatic experience.

✦

½ cup pecans
1½ tablespoons pure maple syrup
½ teaspoon pure vanilla extract
Pinch of ground Ceylon cinnamon
Pinch of freshly grated nutmeg
Ice cubes

Place the pecans, maple syrup, vanilla, cinnamon, and nutmeg in a stand blender, add 1½ cups water, and blend until smooth and creamy.

Strain through a fine-mesh sieve into a shaker. Discard the solids.

Add ice to the shaker and shake vigorously to chill. Strain into two glasses and enjoy.

Choose a Garnish

I like to grate just a little more nutmeg on top.

Dress Your Glass

Coat the rim with honey, then dip in finely crushed pecans.

The Grape Escape

SERVES 1

Looking to escape at the end of a long day? This vibrant mocktail combines the antioxidant power of grapes with the mood-boosting properties of butterfly pea flowers and the calming effects of rosemary and thyme to lead you into your own little safe haven. Butterfly pea flower is one of my favorite herbs to work with because it has a beautiful hue (that actually changes color when exposed to an acid like citrus), offers a natural boost of antioxidants, and promotes cognitive function.

✦

1 heaping teaspoon dried butterfly pea flowers

2 ounces boiling water

¼ cup grapes (any color is okay!)

1 ounce Rosemary Thyme Syrup (page 29)

Juice of ½ lemon (about ½ ounce juice)

Place the butterfly pea flowers in a small bowl or measuring cup and add the boiling water. Steep for at least 5 minutes, or until the water turns a bright blue. Strain through a fine-mesh sieve into a shaker. Discard the solids.

Slice the grapes and add them to the strained tea. Muddle well to release their juices.

Add the syrup and lemon juice to the shaker, fill with ice, and shake vigorously to mix and chill. Dirty pour the mixture (that is, pour the entire contents of your shaker, including ice, without straining) into a glass. If you prefer a smoother drink, strain through a fine-mesh sieve into a glass with fresh ice. Enjoy!

Choose a Garnish

Garnish with a sprig of rosemary and grapes!

Persimmon and Sage Spritz

SERVES 1

This fresh spritz blends the sweetness of persimmons with the earthy flavors of sage and cinnamon, offering functional benefits in every sip. Persimmons are rich in fiber, antioxidants, and vitamin C, which promote digestive health and boost immunity. Sage provides mental clarity and calming effects, while the cinnamon supports digestion and offers anti-inflammatory properties.

✦

2 super ripe persimmons, chopped
2 tablespoons pure maple syrup
1 cinnamon stick
3 to 4 sage leaves
4 ounces orange juice
Juice of 1 lemon (about 1 ounce juice)
Sparkling water

Combine the persimmons, maple syrup, cinnamon stick, and sage leaves in a small saucepan over medium heat. Add ½ cup water and simmer for 10 minutes. Remove from the heat and let cool to room temperature.

Remove and discard the cinnamon stick. Transfer the remaining mixture to a stand blender and blend until smooth. Strain through a fine-mesh sieve into a glass. Discard the solids.

Add the orange juice and lemon juice, mix well, then pour into an ice-filled glass. Top with sparkling water and stir gently to combine.

Tip

There are two prominent types of persimmons, Fuyu and Hachiya. Fuyu is easiest to work with, since it can be used when hard or soft and ripe. Hachiya can be astringent and bitter if it is not super ripe. So if you use Hachiya, make sure it is very ripe!

Choose a Garnish

Garnish with a slice of persimmon, sage, and/or a cinnamon stick.

Dress Your Glass

Coat the rim with honey before dipping in coarse ground sugar.

winter

✦

I grew up in the Sandhills of North Carolina, where snow was a rare and exciting occurrence—one that usually meant school cancellations and weeklong power outages. Some of my fondest childhood memories are of sledding on golf courses, making snow angels, and relishing the stillness that comes with a rare snowstorm. For someone like me, who thrives on energy and activity, the quiet of winter is a reminder to turn inward. This season's reflective nature can be challenging for an active person like me but also deeply restorative—if you allow it. I find comfort in cozying up with a warm drink (and a good book), focusing on self-care, and honoring the space to slow down.

In TCM, winter is associated with the kidneys and the element of water (yin), which governs our vital essence, energy reserves, and strength. It's a time for conservation, replenishment, and rest—preparing for the renewal of spring. The cold naturally draws us inward, making it the perfect time to nourish our bodies with warming, grounding ingredients.

Just like in summer, balancing yin and yang is essential. Since yin is cooling and restorative, these drinks focus on warmth (yang). We use warming and energizing ingredients like pomegranates to support blood circulation (which tends to slow down in winter) and incorporate warming spices like cinnamon and ginger. It's also a great time to lean into dried herbs, teas, and spices, as fresh fruits become less available.

This section is an invitation to embrace the stillness, restore your energy, and savor the comforts of the season.

Ginger Lemon Creamsicle Elixir

SERVES 3 TO 4

This creamy, tangy elixir combines the immune-boosting power of ginger and lemons with the nourishing fats of coconut milk and olive oil. In 2023, an extremely viral lemon olive oil drink took the internet by storm (thanks, @thejenjones), and while I love the original, which uses whole lemons, olive oil, and Ceylon cinnamon, I wanted it to pack an even bigger punch. My version also uses whole lemons, which are rich in vitamin C and antioxidants. Ginger aids digestion, reduces inflammation, and also adds a bit of a kick. Coconut milk provides healthy fats for energy and satiety, and a drizzle of high-quality olive oil adds heart-healthy monounsaturated fats. This drink is pungent, so it's definitely a slow-sipping mocktail! And depending on your flavor palate, it may be something you take more as a wellness shot than a drink.

✦

- 2 lemons, sliced
- Two 2-inch pieces fresh ginger, or more for extra spice
- ¼ cup full-fat canned coconut milk
- 1 tablespoon honey
- Large pinch of sea salt or mineral salt
- High-quality olive oil

Place the lemon slices, ginger, coconut milk, honey, and salt in a stand blender. Add 1 cup water and blend for 30 seconds. You do not want to blend too long or it can become excessively bitter.

Strain through a fine-mesh sieve into glasses.

Drizzle the olive oil over the top of each glass and serve immediately.

Tips

You can store this in the fridge for up to 4 days and drink it as an immune-boosting elixir. For additional sweetness, stir in some honey.

You can use hibiscus tea in place of the water for a fun hue and more herbal goodness. Simply brew 1 tablespoon of hibiscus in 1 cup water for 10 minutes, straining before adding to the blender.

Cranberry Fizz

SERVES 1

This festive mocktail combines tart cranberry juice with the herbal sweetness of rosemary thyme syrup. Cranberries are packed with antioxidants and vitamin C, supporting immunity and heart health, while the syrup adds calming and anti-inflammatory properties. I love serving this drink for celebrations because it is a beautiful color and easy to make a batch for a crowd if you're having a holiday party!

✦

- 1 ounce pure unsweetened cranberry juice
- ½ ounce Rosemary Thyme Syrup (page 29)
- 3 to 4 ounces sparkling water

Combine all the ingredients in a glass and stir well.

Pour into an ice-filled glass and enjoy!

Tip

For an extra festive touch, add cranberries, rosemary, thyme, and water to an ice cube tray, then freeze!

Choose a Garnish

Add a fresh rosemary sprig, fresh thyme sprig, and/or fresh cranberries!

Dress Your Glass

Coat the rim with honey, then dip in coarse sugar or coconut sugar.

Creamy Blood Orange Energizer

SERVES 1

Creamsicle bars are such a delicious and nostalgic treat, so I couldn't wait to make a mocktail version, but with a twist. It's pretty clear I love colorful drinks, but pink drinks have a special place in my heart, which is why I had to use blood orange in this classic riff—but any orange will work! Blood oranges provide a rich source of vitamin C and antioxidants, while green tea offers a gentle caffeine boost and promotes mental clarity. Coconut milk adds healthy fats, and vanilla bean paste creates a dessert-like finish.

✦

1 individual green tea bag
3 ounces hot water (175°F; see Note on page 48)
2 ounces blood orange juice
1 ounce full-fat canned coconut milk
1 teaspoon vanilla bean paste
Pinch of sea salt or mineral salt

Place the tea bag in a small bowl or measuring cup. Add the hot water and let steep for 2 to 3 minutes. Discard the tea bag.

Pour the tea into a shaker, then add the orange juice, coconut milk, vanilla bean paste, and salt. Add ice and shake vigorously to mix and chill.

Strain into a glass filled with fresh ice for a creamy, citrusy treat.

Choose a Garnish

Top with a slice of fresh or dehydrated blood orange.

Dress Your Glass

I love coating the rim in honey, then dipping in flaky coconut to really level it up!

Grapefruit Thyme

SERVES 1

If it isn't clear yet, I'm obsessed with rosemary thyme syrup during the fall and winter months. Its antifungal and anti-inflammatory properties make it as functional as it is flavorful. It pairs perfectly with grapefruit juice for an aromatic and fresh drink that is quite chuggable. Plus, grapefruit is rich in flavonoids, antioxidants, and vitamin C!

✦

2 ounces pure grapefruit juice
1 ounce Rosemary Thyme Syrup (page 29)
Juice of ½ lime (about ½ ounce juice)
Sparkling water

Combine the grapefruit juice, syrup, and lime juice in a glass. Stir well.

Pour into an ice-filled glass and top with sparkling water.

Choose a Garnish

Add a wedge or two of grapefruit and a fresh sprig of thyme or rosemary for an aromatic and elegant touch.

Dress Your Glass

Wet your rim with grapefruit juice or coat with honey. For a sweet herbal rim, dip in a mixture of coarse sugar and thyme or a mixture of grapefruit zest and either flaky salt or coarse sugar (see page 10).

The Cozy Cranberry

SERVES 2

This warming cranberry drink is a perfect balance of tart, sweet, and spiced flavors. Cranberries provide a rich source of antioxidants and vitamin C to support immune health, while blood oranges add a tangy boost of vitamin C and flavonoids. Cinnamon and ginger bring warming, anti-inflammatory properties, and the vanilla bean paste ties everything together with a comforting depth.

✦

Zest and juice of 2 blood oranges
2 cinnamon sticks
One 2-inch piece fresh ginger, sliced
3 ounces pure unsweetened cranberry juice
1 tablespoon vanilla bean paste
Pinch of sea salt or mineral salt
3 tablespoons honey

Combine the orange zest and juice, cinnamon sticks, ginger, cranberry juice, vanilla bean paste, and salt in a small saucepan over medium heat. Add 1 cup water and bring to a simmer.

Reduce the heat to low and simmer for 15 minutes.

Remove from the heat, add the honey, and stir until dissolved.

Strain through a fine-mesh sieve into a glass. Discard the solids. Serve warm, or pour over ice for a refreshing chilled version.

Choose a Garnish

Add a cinnamon stick, dehydrated ginger, fresh cranberries, and/or a slice of blood orange.

Kumquat Smash

SERVES 1

If you love miniature versions of fruit, then you're going to love this drink. I think kumquats are the cutest citrus because they are so small, but they pack a delicious punch of flavor. This drink highlights the unique tart-sweet flavor of kumquats, which are full of vitamin C and antioxidants!

✦

¼ cup quartered kumquats
1 ounce Rosemary Thyme Syrup (page 29)
Juice of ½ lime (about ½ ounce juice)
Pinch of sea salt or mineral salt
Sparkling water

Muddle the kumquats, syrup, lime juice, and salt in a glass to release the kumquats' juices.

Add ice and top with sparkling water. Stir gently and enjoy!

Choose a Garnish

Garnish with a sprig of rosemary or thyme and a few slices of kumquat for an aromatic presentation.

Dress Your Glass

Rub the rim with a slice of lime or coat with honey before dipping in lime zest mixed with flaky salt or coarse sugar (see page 10).

Calming Chamomile Lemonade

SERVES 1

I have a confession. I don't exactly *love* the taste of chamomile, but I do love the benefits. I've also had nutrition and herbal mentors say that not loving an herb may mean you actually need it! So I made this soothing lemonade that combines the calming properties of chamomile with the bright tartness of lemon, in a package that I really enjoy. Chamomile promotes relaxation, reduces anxiety, and supports digestion, while lemon juice provides vitamin C and antioxidants. A touch of honey adds natural sweetness and soothing benefits.

✦

1 tablespoon dried chamomile
4 ounces boiling water
1 teaspoon honey
Juice of 1½ lemons (about 1½ ounces juice)
Pinch of sea salt or mineral salt

Place the dried chamomile in a small bowl or measuring cup and add the boiling water. Let steep for 10 minutes, until the water turns a deep yellow. Strain the chamomile through a fine-mesh sieve into a glass. Discard the solids.

Stir in the honey while still warm to dissolve.

Add the lemon juice and salt, stirring well.

Pour into a glass filled with ice and enjoy a calming, refreshing beverage.

Choose a Garnish

Add a dehydrated lemon slice or a few dried chamomile flowers for an elegant touch.

Dress Your Glass

Rub the rim of the glass with a slice of lime or coat with honey before dipping in lemon zest mixed with flaky salt (see page 10).

Herbal Cranberry Aperol Spritz

SERVES 1

After creating my herbal Aperol syrup, my creativity was popping with all the different ways I wanted to use it . . . because I finally had a way to make different versions of an Aperol spritz! This sophisticated mocktail combines the tartness of cranberry juice with the herbal complexity of an Aperol-inspired syrup. Cranberries offer antioxidants, while orange juice adds vitamin C and sweetness. Adding bitters here introduces an aromatic depth that you expect from an Aperol!

✦

1½ ounces pure unsweetened cranberry juice

1½ ounces Herbal Aperol Syrup (page 25)

1½ ounces orange juice

10 drops bitters

3 ounces sparkling water

Combine the cranberry juice, syrup, orange juice, and bitters in an ice-filled glass. Top with the sparkling water and stir well.

Choose a Garnish

Add a rosemary sprig, orange slice, and fresh cranberries for an aromatic and festive touch.

Cranberry Mandarin Sour

SERVES 1

This vibrant sour isn't a traditional "sour" with a foam top, but considering its flavor profile is pretty dang sour, I just couldn't help but call it a sour. It's loaded with vitamin C and refreshingly tart yet still has the sweetness of mandarin and vanilla.

✦

1½ ounces pure unsweetened cranberry juice
1 ounce mandarin juice
Juice of ½ lemon (about ½ ounce juice)
1 teaspoon vanilla bean paste
Pinch of sea salt or mineral salt
2 ounces sparkling water

Fill a shaker with ice, then add the three juices, the vanilla bean paste, and salt. Shake vigorously to mix and chill.

Strain into a glass filled with fresh ice, then top with sparkling water.

Choose a Garnish

For a polished presentation, add a slice of fresh or dried mandarin and fresh cranberries!

Dress Your Glass

Rub the rim with a slice of lime or coat with honey before dipping in lemon and mandarin zest mixed with flaky salt (see page 10).

Ginger Pomegranate Sour

SERVES 1

This velvety sour combines bold black tea with tart pomegranate juice and the warm, spicy sweetness of ginger honey syrup. Black tea offers antioxidants and a gentle caffeine boost, while pomegranate juice is rich in vitamin C and polyphenols that support heart health. The syrup adds digestive and anti-inflammatory benefits, and the egg white or aquafaba (the liquid from a can of chickpeas) creates a luxurious foam for a creamy texture. You can use pasteurized egg whites if you are concerned about using raw egg whites, and aquafaba is a great vegan option.

✦

1 individual black tea bag
2 ounces boiling water
1 ounce pomegranate juice
1 ounce Ginger Honey Syrup (page 24)
Pinch of sea salt or mineral salt
1 egg white, or 2 tablespoons aquafaba

Place the tea bag in a small bowl or measuring cup and add the boiling water. Let steep 3 to 5 minutes, then discard the tea bag. Let cool slightly.

Combine the tea, pomegranate juice, syrup, salt, and egg white in a shaker.

Dry shake (no ice) to create foam, then add ice and shake again until well chilled.

Pour into a frozen glass and enjoy immediately.

Choose a Garnish

Add a few pomegranate arils or add bitters to the top and swirl.

Elderberry Crush

SERVES 2

This immune-boosting drink highlights the powerful benefits of elderberries combined with the tartness of pomegranate juice and the zesty brightness of lemon. Elderberries are renowned for their antiviral properties and are rich in antioxidants that support overall wellness. Ginger honey syrup adds warmth and aids digestion, while the option to serve hot or sparkling cold makes this drink versatile for any season.

✦

1 tablespoon dried elderberries
2 ounces pomegranate juice
Juice of 1 lemon (about 1 ounce juice)
1 ounce Ginger Honey Syrup (page 24)
4 ounces hot water or sparkling water

Place the dried elderberries in a small saucepan, add 1 cup water, and bring to a boil. Reduce the heat to low and simmer for 10 to 15 minutes.

Remove from the heat and let steep for an additional 5 minutes. Strain through a fine-mesh sieve into a glass to yield about 1 ounce of elderberry tea. Discard the solids.

Add the pomegranate juice, lemon juice, and syrup to the strained tea.

Serve hot or cold. For the hot version, divide the mixture among two mugs, add 2 ounces of hot water to each mug, and stir. For the cold version, divide the mixture into two ice-filled glasses and top each with sparkling water.

Tip

Since elderberry tea needs a slightly longer cooking time, make a large batch of the tea to enjoy throughout the week!

Choose a Garnish

Top with a dehydrated or fresh lemon slice and/or slice of ginger.

Velvet Dreams

SERVES 1

This soothing drink blends the comforting warmth of cinnamon tea with tart cherry juice and creamy vanilla. Tart cherries are rich in melatonin and antioxidants, which promote restful sleep and reducing inflammation. A hint of smoky sea salt enhances the flavors, making this nightcap feel a little indulgent as it lulls you to sleep!

✦

1 individual cinnamon tea bag, or 1 heaping teaspoon ground Ceylon cinnamon

2 ounces boiling water

2 ounces tart cherry juice

1 teaspoon vanilla bean paste

Pinch of smoky sea salt

Place the tea bag in a small bowl or measuring cup and add the boiling water. Let steep for 10 minutes, discard the tea bag, and pour into a glass.

Add the tart cherry juice, vanilla bean paste, and salt. Stir well.

Pour the mixture into a mug and serve immediately for a warm drink. For a cold version, pour into an ice-filled glass.

Choose a Garnish

Add a cinnamon stick and/or a cherry skewer for a decorative finish.

Nonalcoholic Negroni

SERVES 1

When I asked my cocktail-loving friends which drinks they crave during the winter, the Negroni was at the top of the list. This alcohol-free take on a classic Negroni offers the same bold and complex flavors. Pomegranate and cranberry juices provide tartness and antioxidants, while orange juice and zest add a citrusy brightness. A touch of vanilla and warm spices enhances the depth, and chocolate and orange bitters round out the drink with a sophisticated finish.

✦

1½ ounces pomegranate juice
1½ ounces pure unsweetened cranberry juice
2 ounces orange juice
1 teaspoon vanilla bean paste
⅛ teaspoon ground Ceylon cinnamon
⅛ teaspoon orange zest
A few dashes of chocolate bitters
A few dashes of orange bitters

Fill a shaker with ice, then add all the ingredients. Shake vigorously to mix and chill.

Strain into a glass filled with fresh ice.

Choose a Garnish

Add an orange slice, twisted orange peel, cinnamon stick, or even fresh cranberries or pomegranates.

Holiday Punch

SERVES 6

If you need a crowd-pleasing batch mocktail for a party or just so you have extra on hand for yourself, this holiday punch is it. It brings together tart pomegranate, vibrant blood orange, and warm spices for a drink that's worth celebrating. Hibiscus and cardamom add floral and digestive benefits, while cinnamon provides warmth and anti-inflammatory properties.

✦

- 4 cinnamon sticks
- 4 to 5 cardamom pods, slightly crushed
- 1 tablespoon dried hibiscus
- 1 cup pomegranate juice
- ½ cup blood orange juice
- 2 tablespoons vanilla bean paste
- Pinch of sea salt or mineral salt
- Ginger beer or sparkling water (optional)

Combine the cinnamon sticks, cardamom, and hibiscus in a small saucepan, add 2 cups water, and bring to a boil over medium heat. Reduce the heat to low, then simmer for 10 minutes. Strain through a fine-mesh sieve into a punch bowl and let cool. Discard the solids.

Add the pomegranate juice, orange juice, vanilla bean paste, and salt. Stir well, then add ice.

Serve as is or let guests top their drinks with ginger beer or sparkling water.

Choose a Garnish

Set up a DIY garnish station to make this punch interactive and party friendly. I like to serve with sliced blood oranges, cinnamon sticks, cranberries, freshly grated nutmeg, Ginger Honey Syrup (page 24), and/or bitters.

Relaxing Hot Chocolate

SERVES 1

Bone broth hot chocolate goes in and out of favor among online influencers, but the benefits of this one are too great to tamp it down! This luxurious hot chocolate blends rich cacao with adaptogens and nourishing bone broth for a comforting drink with functional benefits. Chaga mushroom helps the body deal with stress and benefits the immune system, while bone broth supports gut health and provides essential nutrients. Cacao is packed with antioxidants and mood-enhancing compounds, and maca root is known for improving mood, making this a warm, indulgent way to unwind.

✦

½ cup bone broth
⅓ cup full-fat canned coconut milk or whole milk
1 tablespoon honey
1 to 2 tablespoons cacao powder
1 teaspoon maca powder
1 teaspoon chaga mushroom powder
1 teaspoon vanilla bean paste
Pinch of sea salt or mineral salt

Bring the bone broth to a simmer in a small saucepan over low heat.

Add the coconut milk, honey, cacao powder, maca powder, chaga mushroom powder, vanilla bean paste, and salt. Stir well to combine. Sometimes I will use a handheld frother to make sure it is thoroughly combined.

Remove from the heat, pour into a mug, and serve.

Choose a Garnish

Top with whipped cream and shaved chocolate for an extra special treat.

Gingerbread White Russian

SERVES 1

The mesmerizing waves of cream meeting coffee will always be alluring to me. This creamy, spiced mocktail delivers the festive flavors of gingerbread in a white Russian, which is a cocktail traditionally made with vodka, a coffee liqueur, and cream. Coffee makes me a little cuckoo, so I love using an herbal coffee alternative to add in liver supportive herbs like dandelion tea. Perfect for cozy evenings or holiday gatherings!

3 ounces freshly brewed coffee or dandelion tea

1 ounce Gingerbread Syrup (page 31)

2 ounces heavy cream (for a dairy-free option, use full-fat canned coconut milk instead)

Combine the coffee with the syrup in a small bowl or measuring cup.

Pour into an ice-filled glass, then top with the heavy cream.

Tip

You can buy loose-leaf dandelion tea at a local apothecary or online, but it is also available in tea bags at most grocery stores.

Choose a Garnish

Sprinkle powdered cinnamon on top and add a cinnamon stick for a festive touch.

Dress Your Glass

Coat the rim with honey, then dip in a mixture of cinnamon, sugar, and ground ginger.

Creamy Chai and Licorice Dessert Mocktail

SERVES 1

This dessert-inspired drink combines the rich spice of chai with the sweet, soothing flavor of licorice. Licorice root supports digestive health and reduces inflammation, but I really love using it for its adaptogenic properties, which support the body's stress response and in turn provide adrenal and hormonal support.

✦

- ½ tablespoon licorice root, or 1 to 2 licorice root tea bags
- 3 ounces boiling water
- 1 ounce Chai Syrup (page 30)
- 2 ounces milk of choice, such as dairy, cashew (page 92), or coconut

Place the licorice root in a small bowl or measuring cup and add the boiling water. Let steep for 7 to 10 minutes, or until the water is light yellow. Strain through a fine-mesh sieve into a glass. Discard the solids.

Add the syrup and milk and stir well.

Pour into a mug and serve immediately for a warm drink. For a cold version, pour into an ice-filled glass.

Choose a Garnish

Top with a star anise and/or a cinnamon stick for an elegant presentation.

Spiced CocoNog

SERVES 1

This tropical twist on eggnog is a creamy and spiced indulgence packed with functional benefits. Coconut provides healthy fats to promote satiety and energy, while black tea offers antioxidants and a gentle energy boost. The warming spices—cinnamon, nutmeg, and cloves—not only evoke holiday coziness but also support digestion, reduce inflammation, and enhance circulation. Vanilla extract and almond extract add depth and sweetness, making this mocktail both sophisticated and nourishing.

✦

1 individual black tea bag
3 ounces boiling water
3 ounces full-fat coconut milk
1 tablespoon sweetened condensed coconut milk
Pinch of ground Ceylon cinnamon
Pinch of freshly grated nutmeg
Pinch of ground cloves
½ teaspoon pure vanilla extract
1 to 3 drops pure almond extract
A few drops of bitters

Place the tea bag in a small bowl or measuring cup and add the boiling water. Let steep for 3 to 5 minutes. Discard the tea bag.

Transfer the tea to a shaker. Add the remaining ingredients along with ice. Shake vigorously to mix and chill.

Pour the mixture into a glass filled with crushed ice and enjoy!

Choose a Garnish

Top with freshly grated nutmeg and a cinnamon stick.

Dress Your Glass

Coat the rim with honey, then dip in flaked coconut.

Simmer Pot Punch

SERVES 4

I love the way a simmer pot fills the house with delicious aromas, but I don't love how wasteful it is, especially when so many of the aromatic ingredients are incredible for your body. You can get really creative with this and make it your own with your favorite fruits and spices. I like cranberries, which are rich in antioxidants that support urinary health; and oranges and apples, which provide immune-boosting vitamin C. The spices—cinnamon, cloves, and star anise—promote digestion and circulation. Rosemary adds a calming, herbal note, while hibiscus and rose hips offer vibrant flavor and a boost of vitamin C. This will make you feel as cozy as your home is going to smell!

✦

½ cup fresh or frozen cranberries
1 orange, sliced
1 apple, sliced
2 to 3 cinnamon sticks
1 tablespoon dried hibiscus and/or rose hips
A few fresh sprigs of rosemary
1 teaspoon whole cloves
1 star anise

Combine all the ingredients in a medium pot, add 4 cups water, and bring to a simmer over medium heat. Let simmer for 10 to 15 minutes to release the flavors and aromas.

Serve warm in mugs, or let cool slightly and pour into ice-filled glasses.

Tip

Make this your own! I also love adding in sliced ginger, lemon, and other aromatic ingredients.

Choose a Garnish

Add orange slices, cranberries, and sprigs of fresh rosemary for a festive presentation.

Toasted Almond Matcha
with Gingerbread Cold Foam

SERVES 1

Over the winter months, I drink a version of this matcha latte almost daily. I love matcha because it is rich in antioxidants and contains the anxiety-reducing amino acid L-theanine and the inflammation-reducing polyphenol compound EGCG (epigallocatechin gallate), making it so good for your body, brain, and skin. Combined with gingerbread syrup, this drink is so cozy and delicious. I also love using my chai syrup with this combo as well. Think gingerbread matcha with a chai cold foam—*yum*! Have fun, get creative, and enjoy!

✦

¼ cup hot water (165°F)

1 teaspoon ceremonial-grade matcha powder

4 ounces Toasted Almond Milk (recipe follows)

2 tablespoons heavy cream or half-and-half

1 ounce Gingerbread Syrup (page 31)

Whisk together the hot water and matcha in a small bowl until frothy. Pour the toasted almond milk into a glass and add the matcha mixture.

In another small bowl or measuring cup, froth the heavy cream with the syrup. Spoon over the matcha and serve.

Dress Your Glass

Coat the rim with honey, then dip in finely chopped toasted almonds.

TOASTED ALMOND MILK

MAKES 4 CUPS

1 cup raw almonds
4 cups filtered water
2 tablespoons pure maple syrup
1 tablespoon vanilla bean paste
Pinch of sea salt or mineral salt

Preheat the oven to 350°F.

Spread out the almonds on a small baking sheet and toast for 5 to 10 minutes, or until the almonds are golden brown. Stir every few minutes for even toasting.

Transfer the almonds to a small bowl, add tap water to cover, and let soak for 6 to 8 hours or up to overnight. Strain through a fine-mesh sieve, then transfer the almonds to a stand blender.

Add the filtered water, maple syrup, vanilla bean paste, and salt and blend. Strain through the sieve into a sealable container.

Storage

Store in the refrigerator for 3 to 5 days.

acknowledgments

Writing this book has been a labor of love, fueled by my passion for creating nourishing drinks and the incredible support of those around me. I couldn't have done this alone, and I am endlessly grateful for the people who helped bring *Everyday Elixirs* to life.

To my love, thank you for taste testing more drinks than you ever expected and giving me brutal honesty, even when I didn't want it. And of course, I couldn't have done this without my faithful kitchen companions, Rose and Archie, the best furry taste testers, who were always hoping for some fruit or even a little carrot to drop on the floor.

Thank you to my friends, who haven't seen as much of me this year but supported me and showed up when I needed you.

Thank you to my absolutely incredible photographer, Joni Schrantz, who not only brought my vision to life but also turned into a great friend during this process. Without your talent, kindness, and friendship, this book wouldn't look nearly as amazing or have been quite as fun to create!

To my editor, Sarah Kwak, and the rest of the team at Harvest, including Jacqueline Quirk, Melissa Lotfy, Shelby Peak, Kimberly Kiefer, Mark Robinson, Anwesha Basu, Liz Psaltis, and Odette Fleming, who were as excited about this book as I was and trusted my vision every step of the way. As a first-time author who didn't know what to expect, you all really made this a joyful and smooth process through all the hard work.

To my literary agents, Callie Deitrick and Wendy Sherman, who have helped me from the very start and stayed present through the entirety. Who needs a bra when I've got a supportive team here to help me succeed!

And of course, to my amazing Holistic Rendezvous community, this book exists because of you. Your excitement for nourishing rituals and your love for these drinks inspired me to create these recipes. Thank you for being part of this journey with me!

This book is a celebration of wellness, joy, and little moments of indulgence. I'm so grateful to everyone who played a part in making it happen. Cheers to you all!

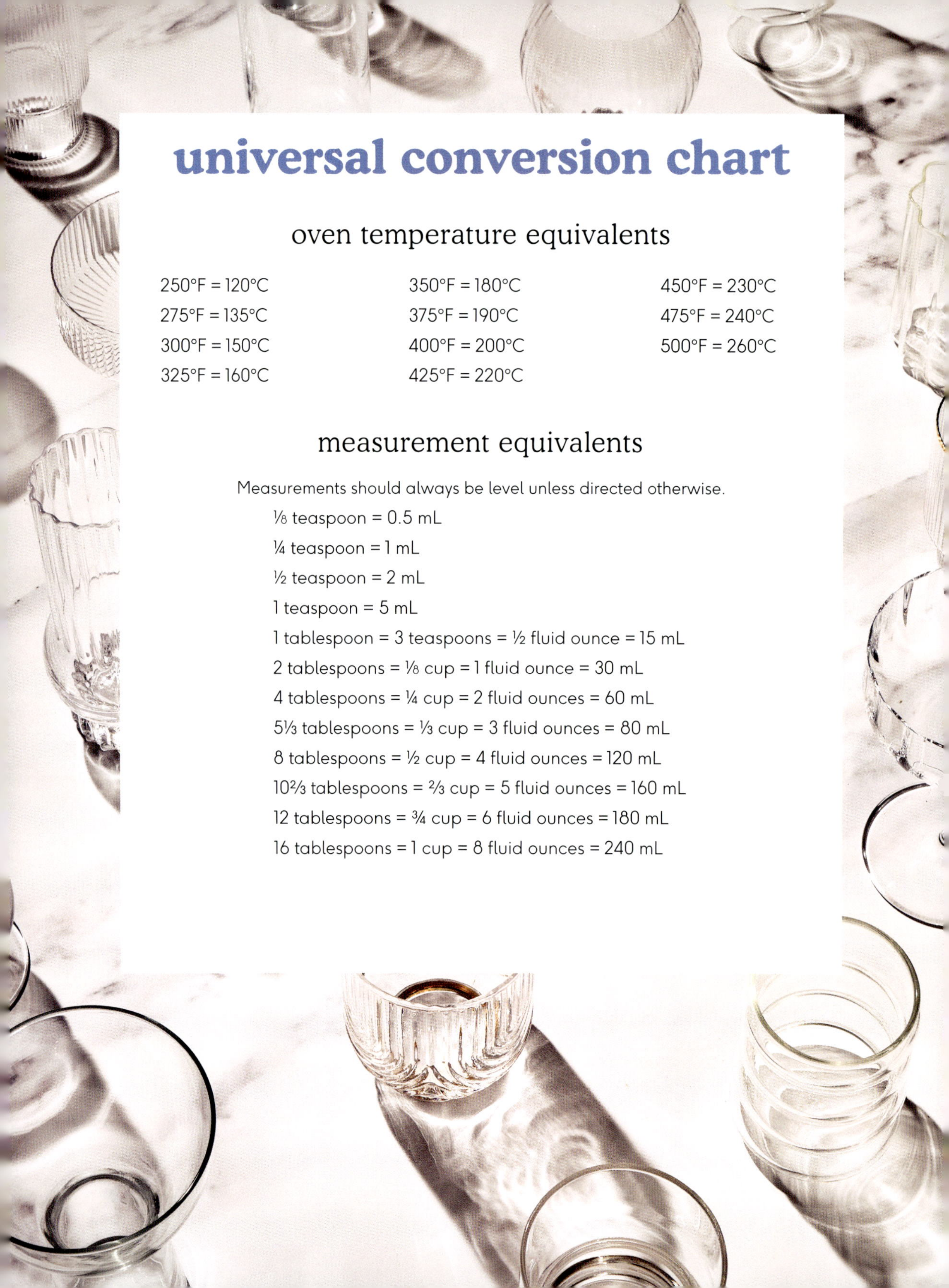

universal conversion chart

oven temperature equivalents

250°F = 120°C
275°F = 135°C
300°F = 150°C
325°F = 160°C
350°F = 180°C
375°F = 190°C
400°F = 200°C
425°F = 220°C
450°F = 230°C
475°F = 240°C
500°F = 260°C

measurement equivalents

Measurements should always be level unless directed otherwise.

⅛ teaspoon = 0.5 mL
¼ teaspoon = 1 mL
½ teaspoon = 2 mL
1 teaspoon = 5 mL
1 tablespoon = 3 teaspoons = ½ fluid ounce = 15 mL
2 tablespoons = ⅛ cup = 1 fluid ounce = 30 mL
4 tablespoons = ¼ cup = 2 fluid ounces = 60 mL
5⅓ tablespoons = ⅓ cup = 3 fluid ounces = 80 mL
8 tablespoons = ½ cup = 4 fluid ounces = 120 mL
10⅔ tablespoons = ⅔ cup = 5 fluid ounces = 160 mL
12 tablespoons = ¾ cup = 6 fluid ounces = 180 mL
16 tablespoons = 1 cup = 8 fluid ounces = 240 mL

Index

Note: Page references in *italics* indicate photographs.

D

E

F

G

M

about the author

Blair Horton is a dynamic force at the intersection of nutrition, holistic health, and artistic expression as a holistic nutrition consultant, certified natural chef and nutrition consultant, and with a degree in applied nutrition. Blair focuses on women's health, hormones, and empowerment and is dedicated to helping women understand their natural cycles and educating them on alternatives to conventional birth control. As a holistic nutrition consultant, Blair empowers women to embrace their well-being through mindful choices and informed decisions.

She immerses herself in recipe and content creation through her business, Holistic Rendezvous, established in 2013. Holistic Rendezvous is more than a business—it's Blair's canvas for self-expression and a gateway to building meaningful connections within the vast landscape of holistic health and nutrition. Blair's work in social media allows her to seamlessly combine her passion for creativity with her dedication to nutrition and health. This passion has not only enabled her to collaborate with remarkable brands but has also fostered a connection with an incredible and supportive online community.

Blair resides in Denver, Colorado, with her boyfriend and their two dogs, Rosey and Archie. Beyond her professional pursuits, Blair is a multifaceted individual with a love for interior design, tennis, pickleball, hiking, and occasionally snowboarding. She finds joy in lifting weights, walking, biking, and teaching high-intensity Pilates a few days a week, engaging with the vibrant Denver wellness community.

This book contains advice and information relating to health care. It should be used to supplement rather than replace the advice of your doctor or another trained health professional. If you know or suspect you have a health problem, it is recommended that you seek your physician's advice before embarking on any medical program or treatment. All efforts have been made to assure the accuracy of the information contained in this book as of the date of publication. This publisher and the author disclaim liability for any medical outcomes that may occur as a result of applying the methods suggested in this book.

 For information, address HarperCollins Publishers, 195 Broadway, New York, NY 10007. In Europe, HarperCollins Publishers, Macken House, 39/40 Mayor Street Upper, Dublin 1, D01 C9W8, Ireland.

HarperCollins books may be purchased for educational, business, or sales promotional use. For information, please email the Special Markets Department at SPsales@harpercollins.com.

hc.com

FIRST EDITION

Designed by Melissa Lotfy

Photography by Joni Schrantz

Library of Congress Cataloging-in-Publication Data has been applied for.

ISBN 978-0-06-343533-9

Printed in Canada.

25 26 27 28 29 TC 10 9 8 7 6 5 4 3 2 1